AF522681

APPROACHES TO MANAGEMENT

APPROACHES TO MANAGEMENT

By

Dr. Elsy P.A

Selection Grade Lecturer
Dept. of Commerce
Vimala College
Thrissur

&

Dr. G. Simon Thattil

Reader
Dept. of Commerce
University of Kerala
Thiruvananthapuram
Kerala-695 034

DISCOVERY PUBLISHING HOUSE PVT. LTD.
NEW DELHI-110 002

First Published-2009

ISBN 978-81-8356-449-6

Published by:
DISCOVERY PUBLISHING HOUSE PVT. LTD.
4831/24, Ansari Road, Prahlad Street
Darya Ganj, New Delhi-110002 (India)
Phone: 23279245 • Fax: 91-11-23253475
E-mail: dphbooks@rediffmail.com
dphtemp@indiatimes.com
web: www.discoverypublishinghouse.com

Printed at:
Sachin Printers
Delhi

Preface

Though management is recognised as an art and a science that originated in the nineteenth or early twentieth century, it has a history that goes back to the origin of man. The records we have on the life of the ancient men clearly show that the ancient society and especially their leaders practised some sort of management. There has been studies on the relatedness of management principles and practices to the Vedas and Vedic philosophy.

In the present study we are approaching the Bible as a record of the ways and means by which the people were organised and brought to growth and development under the leaders sent by God. These leaders have left powerful lessons for the people of our day. To look at the people and their experiences will be of great help to managers of our time. The principles and presuppositions practised by the Biblical leaders stand as a lasting testimony to their deeds. Therefore, a close examination of the performance of the Biblical leaders enables us to pick up principles of management, which are parallel to those applied in modern management.

These have been numerous studies on one or the other aspect of the teachings of the Bible or on Jesus as the founder of the Christian movement. The whole Bible, both the New Testament and Old Testament has not been subjected to a research study from the perspective of Management thought. In the present study the authors are attempting to view the Biblical Perspectives of Management as such. It is not on any part of the Bible, but on the Biblical perspectives in general.

The Central characters in this book are Moses and Jesus Christ.

Moses is the manager in the Old Testament and his influence is felt from the beginning till the end of the Old Testament period. Jesus is the leader par excellence and the whole New Testament resounds with his words and deeds. Both these leaders – Moses and Jesus can also be liberators or leaders of liberation movement. In fact the whole Bible, both the Old Testament and the New Testament is the story of a liberation movement under two perspectives, the first (Old Testament) under the perspective of God's special grace in favour of the Jewish people and the second (New Testament) under the perspective of God's universal love for humankind. These two individuals and the principles, which guided them in their contribution, as leaders to the movement are the special questions, treated in this study. These two leaders are not looked upon from the perspective of theology or spirituality as such, but from the point of view of management, the modern art and science, which attract thousands of young men and women to the world universities.

Thus Moses stands as the foundation of the organised life of the Jewish people. It is this man that we have taken for our research study. Since Moses is the foundation, our findings apply to the whole old Testament.

From the New Testament we have taken the life of Jesus for our research. Jesus is the one leader who is normative for all that we read in the New Testament. He is the founder of the New Testament religion called Christianity. He is the model after which every other New Testament leader wants to form himself or herself. He is the ideal to which all the Books of the New Testament are inviting the readers. Therefore this normative character of Jesus makes him the leader, the only leader or the leader par excellence of the New Testament. It is this Jesus that forms the second personality for our study. Thus this study takes into account the whole ideal of management set forth in the whole Bible.

This study does not stop with picking up the management principles applied by Moses and Jesus. Over and above these principles the research looks into the hidden power that functioned as the foundation and source of these leaders. Therefore this research goes beyond the visible aspects of management to a realm that lies beyond the reach of empirical, scientific study of management. Thus this study adds a new dimension to management study. Mc Kenzie's 7-S approach and looking beyond that is the theme researched. This further adds to the relevance of the study. The findings of the study are presented in this book as a humble effort to project our how such principles were used even before the discipline of Management emerged.

—Authors

Contents

Preface

1. **A Short History of Management Thought** 1
   - — Management and Administration
   - — The Five Stages of Development
     - – First Stage–The Scientific Approach
     - – Second Stage–Emphasis on Human Relationship in Management
     - – Third Stage–Social Sciences and Management
     - – Fourth Stage–Management as a Science by Itself
     - – Fifth Stage–Integrated Management Thought (Present Stage)

2. **Different Approaches to Management** 53
   - — Case Approach
   - — Inter-personal Behavioural Approach
   - — Group Behaviour Approach
   - — Co-operative Social Systems Approach
   - — Composite Longwall Method Approach
   - — Decision Theory Approach
   - — Systems Approach
   - — Quantitative or Mathematical Approach
   - — Contingency Approach
   - — Managerial Roles Approach
   - — Management Process Approach

3. **The Seven-S Approach** 74

— Researches Leading to Seven-S Approach
  – The Concept of Excellence
— The Different items in the Seven-S Approach
  – Strategy
  – Structure
  – System
  – Style
  – Staff
  – Shared Values
  – Skill

4. **The Seven-S Approach in the Bible** 101

The Seven-S Approach in the Liberation Movement of Moses
— Strategy
— Structure
— System
— Style
— Staff
— Shared Values
— Skills

5. **Seven-S Approach in the Life of Jesus** 127

— Strategy of Jesus
— Structure
— System
— Style
— Staff
— Shared Values
— Skills

6. **Beyond Seven-S** 158

— The Limitations
  – The Naming

- The Numbering
- Is Shared Value Possible?
- Charismatic Quality
- Learning and Applying Skills
- Affiliative Interest
- Spirituality and Management
- Ethics

— The Recognition of the Divine in the Human
- Mother Teresa
- John Paul II

— The Beyond in the Biblical Management
- The Beyond in Moses' Management
- The Beyond in Jesus' Management

7. **General Conclusion** **173**

Bibliography *183*

Index *201*

1

A Short History of Management Thought

Management as a science and profession is perhaps less than a century old, but as a practice it is as old as mankind. There has been extensive research on the various evolutionary practices of Management and its references in ancient epics and literature.

In the present study we are approaching the Bible as a record of the ways and means by which the people were organised and brought to growth and development under the leaders sent by God. These leaders have left powerful lessons for the people of our day. To look at the people and their experiences will be of great help to managers of our time. The principles and presuppositions practised by the Biblical leaders stand as a lasting testimony to their deeds. Therefore, a close examination of the performance of the Biblical leaders enables us to pick up principles of management, which are parallel to those applied in modern management.

There have been numerous studies on one or the other aspect of the teachings of the Bible or on Jesus as the founder of the Christian movement. The whole Bible, both the New Testament and Old Testament has not been subjected to a research study from the perspective of Management thought. In the present study the authors are attempting to view the Biblical Perspectives of Management as such. It is not on any part of the Bible, but on the Biblical perspectives in general. The Central characters in this book are Moses and Jesus Christ.

Moses is the manager in the Old Testament and his influence is felt from the beginning till the end of the Old Testament period. Jesus is the leader par excellence and the whole New Testament resounds with his words and deeds. Both these leaders – Moses and Jesus can also be liberators or leaders of liberation movement. In fact the whole Bible, both the Old Testament and the New Testament is the story of a liberation movement under two perspectives, the first (Old Testament) under the perspective of God's special grace in favour of the Jewish people and the second (New Testament) under the perspective of God's universal love for humankind. These two individuals and the principles, which guided them in their contribution, as leaders to the movement are the special questions, treated in this study. These two leaders are not looked upon from the perspective of theology or spirituality as such, but from the point of view of management, the modern art and science, which attract thousands of young men and women to the world universities.

Thus Moses stands as the foundation of the organised life of the Jewish people. It is this man that we have taken for our research study. Since Moses is the foundation, our findings apply to the whole Old Testament.

From the New Testament we have taken the life of Jesus for our research. Jesus is the one leader who is normative for all that we read in the New Testament. He is the founder of the New Testament religion called Christianity. He is the model after which every other New Testament leader wants to form himself or herself. He is the ideal to which all the Books of the New Testament are inviting the readers. Therefore this normative character of Jesus makes him the leader, the only leader or the leader par excellence of the New Testament. It is this Jesus that forms the second personality for our study. Thus this study takes into account the whole ideal of management set forth in the whole Bible.

This study does not stop with picking up the management principles applied by Moses and Jesus. Over and above these principles the research looks into the hidden power that functioned as the foundation and source of these leaders. Therefore this research goes beyond the visible aspects of management to a realm that lies beyond the reach of empirical, scientific study of management. Thus this study adds a new dimension to management study. Mc Kenzies's 7-S approach and looking beyond that is the theme researched. This further adds to the relevance of the study. The findings of the study are presented in this book as a humble effort to project our how such principles were used even before the discipline of Management emerged.

The book is an outcome of the research work undertaken by the authors as the presentation is in two parts.

In the first part we are exclusively dealing with the art and science of management. This will function as the foundation for the next part, which deals with management as practices by the leaders of the Bible. We will first look into the history of management, the different stages through which it developed and attained the present status. Then we will go to the different approaches to the management. This will lead us to the widely used approach namely 'The Seven-S approach', which is accredited as the most important. There we will speak of the seven items, which constitute the Seven-S approach. The two famous books namely *'The Art of Japanese Management'* and *'In Search of Excellence'* are specially used for arriving at the excellence of this approach.

Objectives of the Study

The main objectives of the study are:

1. To trace the Biblical teachings on references to managerial principles, thoughts and practices.
2. To identify Leadership Models and Human Relations Models of modern management which had their Biblical roots.

3. To compare and contrast the different management approaches and to establish the relationship between the Biblical approach and the Seven-S approach of McKenzie.
4. To identify role models, as depicted in the Bible and assess their qualities and capabilities so as to examine whether they do have relevance in contemporary management.
5. To ascertain whether theories of management relating to leadership styles, human behaviour, organisational systems and value systems had a Biblical origin in terms of application in certain contexts.

Methodology

The study is theoretical in nature and is conducted in two parts. Part one includes analysing the origin and growth of management thought. The evolution of management study up to the twenty first century is covered here. The second part is based on Biblical literature having reference to managerial styles, systems and theories. The focus of the study in this part is to identify cases, instances and anecdotes, which apply management principles in actual life.

The Seven-S approach is the most recent and widely accepted approach to management. I proceed with this presupposition. There are many recent management thinkers who have contributed highly for management studies. We examine these writers.

With the insights collected from these most recent management thinkers we go back to the two leaders of the Bible and bring out the amazing parallelism between them and the recent management thinkers. The uniqueness in the approaches adopted by these leaders and its relatedness to the Seven-S model is examined in detail. This unique aspect we call 'faith in an Absolute Being', a true faith that is expressed in practical life. This finding is further examined with the lessons gathered from the most recent world leaders. We pick up two such persons – Mother Teresa and Pope John Paul II whose origins are too humble, yet were able to attract more people as their disciples and admirers than any other leader with esteemed origins and solid background. The success of these two leaders also points to the same fact as the uniqueness in the leaders taken from the Bible. They had faith as the source and foundation from which they gathered strength to perform successfully in their respective fields.

LITERATURE RELATING MANAGEMENT WITH RELIGION AND SPIRITUALITY

It is interesting to note that in recent years many scholars have found amazing parallelism between scientific management and the way the religions and the various sects within the religion are organised. In this regard the scriptures, which provide the basic principles of the religion, present a lot of persons, either historical or fictional as able managers. The same way the rules and the organisation of some of the religious congregations within the Catholic Church show an amazing parallelism with modern management approach. These have been subjected to research study by some of the eminent scholars in this field. As this study is of the same nature I will note down some of these writers with short comments on their contributions.

Adebowale Akande: In an article (1991)[1] he discusses the relationship between human resources management practices and organisational characteristics of Biblical personalities such as competitive strategy, analysis and technology. Pointing out the example of Joseph of the Old Testament who was appointed by pharaoh of Egypt as his prime minister the author indicates the necessity of appointing a significant leader in the management team on certain occasions. He also comments that changes in the business environment demand a faster-paced approach to human resource planning. The story of Joseph is given as an example.

Braam Oberholster: In a short study (1993)[2] presentation he gives an overall view of management from a Biblical perspective. According to him the notion of management as introduced by the Bible, centres on the concept of stewardship. The Christian management works for people within a system, and meets their psychological, social, intellectual, aesthetic, and spiritual needs while addressing economic, technological, societal, and environmental concerns in a harmonious response that benefits all and brings glory to God. If one responds to this idea by saying: "Impossible, no human agent can then successfully exercise management", the author claims that he has succeeded in making clear that without the help of God successful management is impossible. He also says that we have to realign our measurement of success to the biblical perspective. We often limit the measurement of results to quantitative success measures (be it financial, market share or pass in examination) to determine success, but we need to understand that the true measurement of success for the biblical steward was his relationship with God and humans.

Donald W. McCormick: American managers show increasing interest in integrating spirituality and management and this integration offers managers a source of enduring meaning in turbulent times. Donald W. McCormick is one such American scholar. In an article (1994)[3] he examines the values, tasks and problems of managers that emerge as common themes in different spiritual paths.

Laurie Beth Jones (1994 & 2001): *Jesus, CEO: Using Ancient Wisdom for Visionary Leadership* (1994)[4] is her main book on management. She highlights three ideas which we can pick up from Jesus' management style.

1. One person trained twelve human beings who went on to influence the world. By this movement time itself is now recorded as being before (B.C.) or after (A.D.) his existence.

2. This person worked with a staff that was totally human and not divine ... a staff that in spite of illiteracy, questionable backgrounds, fractious feelings, and momentary cowardice went on to accomplish that task he trained them to do.

3. His leadership style was intended to be put to use by any of us.

This author calls the management style of Jesus as "Omega" style which incorporates and transcends the best of the Alpha (masculine) and Beta (feminine) leadership styles, because she believes that by harnessing spiritual energy, each of us, female and male, can become the empowered leaders that the third millennium will require. The same author has also written another book by name "Jesus, Entrepreneur" (2001)[5] which tells that beyond work and beyond entrepreneurism, there is "spiritreneurism" – work that allow you to do well by doing right. In *Jesus, Entrepreneur* Laurie Beth Jones shows how to find soul satisfaction in work. She shows that there is no contradiction between earning a comfortable living even as you use your job to promote your deepest spiritual and personal beliefs. This is possible by sharing timeless wisdom from the Bible in today's rapidly changing business environment. She reminds all of us that the be–all and end-all of any truly successful spiritreneur's work is love – the kind of love that transcends all toil, all tears, and all time.

Anthony Scaperlanda: In an article (1998)[6] that reviews the three encyclicals of Pope John Paul II namely *Laborem Exercens, Sollicitudo Rei Socialis and Centesimus Annus* he affirms that the papal documents have Biblical and theological insights and that they can add another voice to the discussion of the oversight of multinational enterprises.

Rick L. Edgeman: In an article (1998)[7] he understands leadership as a fusion of ethical core values, competencies and empowerment. Organisations devote a great deal of attention to the cultivation and deployment of competencies, which support their mission and vision. Of equal importance, but less-attended to— are core values for cultures and economies rise and fall on the basis of these foundations. One core value, which is consistently included in the criteria of various international quality prizes, is that of employee empowerment. Coupled with enabling competencies and profound trust, fully deployed core values allow empowerment to be taken to its extreme logical conclusion – systemic leadership wherein all members of an organisation share the burdens, privileges, and rewards of leadership. Leadership is regarded as a key enabler of business excellence. Leadership as developed in this paper fuses ethical core values, competencies, and empowerment. Effective deployment results in systemic leadership that is marked by unity of purpose, which in turn facilitates the journey to business excellence.

Michael Henry Kennedy: This author makes a comparative study of the Rule of St. Benedict, written for the guidance of the running of monasteries and Henry Fayol's principles of Management. The comparative study is enshrined in an article written by him in 1999[8]. The Rule of St. Benedict was written in the sixth century while Fayol's principles came in the twentieth century. The parallelism between them shows that the basic principles of management were already in use in all ancient human organisations.

Low Sui Pheng: This author looks into the Bible with the eye of a manager. His findings are given expression in an article written in 1999[9]. He highlights the basic guiding principles, which are laid down in the Holy Bible and affirms that these are to be taken into serious consideration in modern management approach because these are of eternal value. He suggests that modern management concept should be synthesised with the guiding principles of the Bible to attain managerial efficacy.

Rabbi Baron: His is a study of Moses, the liberator of the Jewish people who managed the liberation movement with insights which are still valid and applicable to the modern man. By an indepth study of the managerial approach of Moses, the author lays down fifty powerful lessons for today's business managers. Some of the most important lessons suggested in the book (2000)[10] are: (1) how to bring the staff out of the slavish mentality; (2) The importance of face to face negotiation to bring about optimum results; (3) How crises can be used as open door to change. There are many other such lessons which are useful for modern managers.

N.M. Khandelwal: The author brings to light the managerial approaches enshrined in the ancient epic by name Mahabharata. This is a research study (2001)[11]. He shows that the leaders of the Kurukshethra war like Krishna, Bhishma,

Duryodhana were having advanced knowledge of management. In fact the modern science of management is only old wine in new wineskins.

Anthony A. D'Souza: In a book entitled 'Leaders for Today Hope for Tomorrow'[12] the author gives an overall picture of Jesus' leadership styles on different occasions. With the power of the Word of God, with the persuasion of vivid parables and with the poignancy of his own life example, he taught the disciples how to lead his people. He showed them leadership as service, compassionate service. There are three striking and recurrent Biblical images of leadership in the New Testament, all beginning with the letter 'S': Servant, Shepherd and Steward. The author comments that following the example of Jesus one must treat others with respect, justice, fairness and love. One's actions will manifest to the world around him/her God's love, justice and caring.

Easo John: The main concern of this author is to point out the irreconcilable difference between the Christian conscience and the divines on modern managers. According to him the moral values enshrine in the Bible have a universal validity, which are binding on every human being. But a modern manager finds it impossible to live according to these principles. According to him the core of management education should aim at "broadening of the mind with emphasis on the ability to analyse problems and situations, and building the ability to look at alternate solutions with all their implications to all facets of business."[13]

Gregory Stone A., Robert F. Russel and Kathleen Patterson: In an article (2004)[14] co-authored by these three scholars they examine transformational leadership and servant leadership and bring out the similarities and differences between them. The transformational leadership focuses on the organisation while the other focuses on the followers. The authors suggest that these two kinds of leadership should function together in an organisation to make leadership itself dynamic.

Lorin Woolfe: This author provides a unique way to view the Bible and considers the reasons behind the success of Moses, Joseph and others of the Bible in a study by name *The Bible on Leadership* (2005)[15]. Joseph rises to the seat of power through his political skill, John the Baptist was a wonderful communicator. Queen Esther could achieve what she wanted through political know-how. Compassion and communication skill are behind the success of Jesus. These are some of the leadership principles the author picks up from the Bible. These are presented as valid and useful for modern managers.

SCHOOLS OF MANAGEMENT THOUGHT

Management as a scientific discipline to be taught in colleges and universities is of recent origin. But the practice of management is very old. How old is it? J.S. Chandan says, "Even though the formal scientific management practise began and established itself in the early part of the 20th century the recorded application of organised management dates back to 5000 B.C. when Sumerians established written records for both government and commercial use. As early as 3000 B.C. Egyptians were aware of the importance of planning, directing, organising, and controlling and this is evident from the great pyramids of Egypt, built around 2800 B. C."[16]

But this is about the recorded history of human species and the evidence of application of managerial principles in the life of the humans. But we cannot think that the practice of management started only with the beginning of recorded history. It is now evident that the humans lived millions of years before they invented the art of writing. In this non-recorded past also management was practised. This means the practice of management is as old as the age of the human species. We are not sure of the origin of the human species on the earth.

There are different theories about the origin of man and the most prominent among them are theories of monogenesis and polygenesis.[17] Monogenesis says that humanity originated from a first man created by God. This is the theory mostly accepted by the religious minded people especially the Christians. But here also the idea is that humanity originated from the first human couple. That means already in the very first stage of human history there are at least two persons—a man and a woman. For them to live together in harmony there was need for some sort of management. That means we cannot conceive of a human history without one individual taking the leadership, guiding and controlling the other or others.

If we are to subscribe to polygenesis, then the supposition is that many individuals evolved into human species from previous non-human species. Therefore, in this supposition there is already a society not simply an individual or family; and if that society survived the test of time to become a sophisticated society, we have to presuppose that there were leaders among them who guided and controlled the other members of the society. Therefore, we are correct in claiming that the art and practice of management is as old as the age of the human species itself.

Management and Administration

Before we go into the history of management it is important to clarify the difference between the two concepts namely management and administration. There is a widespread misconception that management is nothing but administration. It is true that management and administration are interrelated disciplines; but they are not identical. There are a few people who think that administration is a broad activity while management is a narrow one. It is mainly the American writers like Tead, Shulze, Oliver Scheldon, William Spriegal etc who have made this distinction between management and administration. "For them management was only an executive function, getting things done."[18] For example G.E. Milward distinguishes administration and management in the following way.

> Administration is primarily the process and the agency used to establish the object or purpose, which an undertaking and its staff are to achieve. Secondly administration has to plan and stabilise the broad lines of principles, which will govern action. These broad lines are in their turn usually called policies. Management is the process and the agency through which the execution of policy is planned and supervised.[19]

In this distinction management is reduced to a narrow activity coming under the broad perspective of administration. Many other writers followed this trend. For example T. Ramasamy identifies six basic distinctions between administration and management. In his distinctions the main focus is on the directness of the activity of the manager against the theoretical and mediate nature of the function of administrator. According to him the administrator acts as a principal while the manager acts as the agent. The administrator plans, organises and staffs while the manager directs, motivates and controls. In this distinction the manager is the one who stands in touch with achieving the desired results. The other functions like planning, organising are attributed to the administrator.[20] He also thinks that the administrative functions belong to the owners or board of directors and this function is the top-level executive function. The manager stands at a lower level. This distinction also does not stand to the actual experience of managers today. In modern times the manager is called upon to do whatever is needed for the achievement of the aim. As V.P. Michael has correctly observed.

> In several organisations administrative job is also looked after by respective functional managers, and they do not feel the need for an administrative man, while at least some managers believe that an administrative position is unnecessary. In certain organisations the top manager himself may be looking after the administrative functions also, while he himself may be the policy maker.[21]

This observation is very much in line with the experience of many firms and organisations. This observation goes against the idea that management is something that comes under administration. The fact is just the opposite. Administration, very often comes under management. The owner of a firm need not always be a successful administrator. All that he contributes for the firm or organisation may be the financial investment he makes. But money kept by itself is dead and does not make any profit. The manager on the other hand may be doing all the work related to the functioning of the firm.

This analysis of the two functions—management and administration—makes it clear that they are not identical functions. Administration is one thing and supervision is quite another thing. Yet they are complimentary and co-related. If we interrelate these two functions management is to be understood as more generic and administration as more specific.

> Management represents the whole system while administration is a subsystem of the management system. Similarly, if management is considered as a profession, administration is only a function of that profession. From a personified angle management can be considered as a class while administration is only an activity of that class. Similarly, management is academically viewed as either a science or an art. In both the cases administration is a tool.[22]

In the process of the development of management from its initial stage as a necessary practice for social life to the stage of becoming a science by itself, it has travelled a long distance and received contributions from many thinkers and scientists. As Donnelly says:

> Between the two extremes of management practice and management science are many individuals who have contributed to the study of management. They include engineers, sociologists, psychologists, anthropologists, lawyers, economists, accountants, mathematicians, political scientists, and philosophers.[23]

In places where people worked together there was need for a manager who directed and co-ordinated the activities of the various members. Even in a small supermarket with five or six sales personnel there is the need of a manager who directs them. But in the pre-mechanisation era the number of workers in a firm was limited and the one who is put in charge of the workers could direct them without any previous scientific knowledge of what management was. The personal talents of the manager, power of his word, the respect he enjoyed among the workers etc were enough for him to function as an efficient manager. These managers managed the companies without being aware that they were practising a very complicated art and science.

With mechanisation and the emergence of large factories where hundreds and thousands of workers from different cultural backgrounds worked together in different shifts all through the 24 hours of the day, the personal qualities acquired without any formal training became insufficient. People felt the need for formal training and planned direction of the firm in order to bring about the desired results. It is this situation, which necessitated Management to be taken seriously and proper training is to be given to the managers for successful functioning.

The Five Stages of Development

When we look into the history of formal management studies we can identify at least four stages in its history. This history is a long one going back to more than one hundred years. The development of management thought has achieved during these more or less one-century may be seen in these four stages. The first stage is the beginning of scientific study of management. This is the period from 1880 to 1930. The second one is the study of management with stress on human relationship and this period may be specified between 1930 and 1950. The third stage is the period when social sciences began to influence management studies. This is roughly the period from 1950 to the present time. We can identify a fourth stage and that is the period when management is looked upon as a science like any other social science like sociology, economics and anthropology. The beginning of this stage is almost identical with the period of the third stage. We may analyse these different stages one by one as follows.

The Beginnings

Earlier we spoke about the origin of management as coinciding with the history of social life of humans. In this regard some of the organised institutions of the ancient world deserve special mention. These organisations may be understood as paths leading to the scientific era of management though these organisations themselves cannot be termed scientific in a formal sense. Historians tell us that the administration of life in the ancient cities of Aryan civilisation in the beginning of 2nd millennium B.C. was well organised and properly planned. Mohanjadhara and Harappa, which are living monuments of the great achievements of the ancient Indians, cannot be imagined except as the result of organised effort and proper planning. In this regard the visionary endeavours of the Buddhists towards the end of the 1st half of the first millennium also deserve special mention. If the enlightenment of the Buddha could be communicated to the people in the remote Asian cities of the time it was because of planned effort and organised apostolate. In the West we have the example of the great Greek cities. A sort of democracy existed in these cities. These also were the result of well organised planning and effort. The Roman Catholic Church, which stood the test of time, is another example of planning and organisation. But these are not scientific management in the modern sense.

By the 2nd half of the eighteenth century, with mechanisation and industrial revolutions people felt the need for change in their management concepts to cope up with the new situation in the world. This period may be considered as the immediate situations leading to scientific management thought. During the transition period the contribution of some economists was of great value. They have influenced later thinkers to evolve scientific concepts of management. The contributions of Adam Smith[24], J.S. Mill[25], James Mill[26], J.B. Say[27], Samuel P. Newman[28], W.S. Jevons[29] and others are very great. In the field of management itself mention is to be made of Robert Owen[30], Charles Babbage[31] and Henry R. Towne[32] who are considered to be pre classical contributors to management study. Robert Owen insisted on the human element in management. Even if all the material conditions are ideal one cannot expect the desired result unless the workers contribute their share of the productivity. The workers are to be treated humanly and with confidence. "He strongly emphasised the need for the manager to take the worker into his confidence and should not only tell him what is expected of him, but also why, because an enlightened worker is a better worker."[33] The workers should be made to work not because they have to work but because they like the work. This means a situation is to be created in which the workers feel the enthusiasm in the work.

Robert Owen's "Ideas and philosophy could be considered as a prelude to the development of the behavioural approach to management."[34]

Charles Babbage was more of a mathematician than a manager by profession. He is considered as the father of modern computing. Almost in the same line with Owen, he advocated the importance of human factor in management. His special contribution is his insistence on sharing profit with the workers and giving them participation in decision making. He proposed that labour should be properly divided and workers intelligently organised. Another management thinker is Towne. His main contribution is that he insisted on the development of management concepts and skill as a discipline. In later times F.W. Taylor developed Towne's ideas in a systematic way and earned for himself the fame as the 'father of scientific management'.

The forerunners to scientific management have made considerable contributions through their direct involvement in management and through their writings. Yet their contributions are not considered scientific.

> These contributions were made bit by bit in a haphazard manner. They mainly comprise stray thoughts of some individuals focussing attention on different aspects of management. However, their studies were not systematic. It was mainly based on hunches and some experiences.[35]

First Stage—The Scientific Approach

In the first stage the most significant contribution of management thinkers is the development of management principles in the practise of management. They made a conscious effort to raise the status of management to the level of a scientific discipline. But what is a discipline itself and what is a science? A discipline may be described as that which "refers to a field of study having well defined concepts and principles."[36] Science may roughly be defined as a system "having clear concepts, theory and other accumulated knowledge developed from hypotheses (assumptions that something is true), experimentation and analysis."[37] Scientific management is "that kind of management which conducts a business or affairs by standards established by facts or truths gained through systematic observation, experiment, or reasoning."[38]

There can be the question whether management is a science or an art. Management is doing things and not simply having theoretical knowledge of things. Therefore, it is an art of the same nature as the practices like medicine, music, engineering, literary writing etc. These practices are arts; almost in the same way management also is an art. What is an art itself? As the Oxford dictionary defines, art is the "skill in doing anything as the result of knowledge and practice."[39] Art is basically concerned with the practical. But the practices become systematic and receive the status of an art when they have the backing of systematic knowledge or science. "If science teaches one to know art teaches one to do."[40] Therefore, we can say without doubt that management is both a science and an art.

The statement that management is an art and a science needs further explanation. When we say management is a science we do not mean that it is a science like physics, chemistry etc. These are positive sciences. But management is not a positive science. Yet it is a science. To explain let us go to a clear idea of science itself. Science is that which works on universally valid principles. The physical law that every action has an equal and opposite reaction is universally true. Such universally true principles cannot be expected in every aspect of management. In fact four are the elements that come under the functions of management. A manager manages business, managers, work and workers. Of these four, two are things, namely, business and work. The two others, managers and workers are persons. The principles that are applicable to things are not equally applicable with regard to persons. About the functioning of things, we can have universally valid principles. Therefore, from that aspect of management, it has a scientific status. But management has also to do with people. We cannot have a mechanical approach to man. "Men are complex living organisms having emotional responses and also influenced by the external macro conditions...the external behaviour of men may not always be as the managers desire."[41] There is the need for developing the art of dealing with men. But the unpredictable nature of men cannot be over-emphasised to the extend of making it impossible for the manager to deal with them. With the aid of sociology and social psychology and other related sciences, the manager can deal with people in such a way that they are made to bring about the desired result. Yet it is a skill to manage people. Therefore from the point of view of the human factor of management it is more of the nature of an art; from the point of view of things, which the manager has to deal with, management is more of a scientific nature. In conclusion, we can say that management is both an art and a science. Where the science of management stops, the art begins.

> Facts are first used, "knowns" are given preference and data on tangibles are considered. These scientific aids are pursued to their limits, but in any given case they may seem inadequate. It is then that the manager must turn to artistic managerial ability to perform a job.[42]

Some Important Contributors in the First Stage

The contributions of earlier thinkers like Robert Owen, Charles Babbage and Henry Robinson Towne were not sufficient to make management a scientific discipline. These contributors may be regarded as a forerunner to the systematic or scientific management thought. An integrated effort to study management in a systematic manner came to the mind of management thinkers only when the industrial and commercial revolution started to affect the political, social and economic life of people. It paved the way to a new era in the history of management. Among the various thinkers who took management as a serious issue and made an investigation to bring it to the status of a scientific discipline include Frederic Winslow Taylor, Henry Laurence Gantt, F.B. Gilbreth, Mrs.Gilbreth and Henry Fayol. The main contributions of each of these management thinkers can be seen in the following pages.

Frederic Winslow Taylor

F.W. Taylor pioneered the scientific management concept in the period between 1880 and 1930. He is known as the father of scientific management. His main contribution to management studies is given expression in his famous works which are: (1) *Shop Management* published in 1903; (2) *Principles of Scientific management* published in 1911; and (3) *Testimony Before the Special House Committee* (1912).[43] He realised by his observation and experiments in factories that the methods of production lacked planning and that the tools and equipments used were meagre and odd. The reason was that work and working methods were not organised well. Based on his experience in US steel industry, he put forward a precise approach to the problems of work and work organisation. Two of his experiments are world famous. At the Bethlehem Steel Company he conducted thousands of stopwatch observations of the performance of the workers. He watched the way the various shovelers pushed their shovels into the pile of coal, how they swung the shovels and how they threw the loads. Another experiment was with pig iron handling. From these observations he came to certain scientific conclusions, which were later followed, by other writers and contributors to management studies. It was his firm conviction that the proper organisation of the workforce and work methods would improve efficiency. He challenged both managers and workers for a mental and attitudinal revolution. He believed that work is the result of a co-operative effort between managers and workers. So work should be organised in such a way that worker is left with his own particular task only and not with any other responsibility. This will enable him to concentrate on and specialise in his particular work and make him perfect in his job.

The job observation and job analysis led to a precise performance standard and a best performance method was arrived at. This was beneficial to all – to the organisation, managers and workers. It is beneficial to the organisation because it eliminates all wasteful and inefficient use of resources. For the managers also it is beneficial because they can set out and demand some standard of work from workers. In other words, it stimulated managements into adopting a more positive and constructive role in leadership at the shop-floor level. It is beneficial for workers because they can concentrate and become experts in their particular work. Besides, it forced the management to improve the physical working conditions for employees. From financial point of view also everyone would benefit from the standardisation of products, increase in output, sales and profits and this will lead to increase in the level of wages and salary.[44]

As he himself states: "the principal object of management should be to secure maximum prosperity of the employer coupled with the maximum prosperity for the employee."[45] To achieve this, he developed standardisation, time and motion studies, functional foremanship, production planning and control, piece-wage system of differential basis etc.[46]

Taylor's suggestions can be listed as follows:

- Replacement of Rule of Thumb with science or organised knowledge.
- Ensuring harmony, which promotes give-and-take situation in group action rather than discord.
- Achieve co-operation, confidence and goodwill among management and workers instead of chaotic individualism. Taylor has suggested "substitution of war for peace, hearty and brotherly co-operation for contentment and strife, replacement of suspicious watchfulness with mutual confidence, of becoming friends instead of enemies. It is along this line, I say, that scientific management must be developed."[47]
- Obtain maximum output in place of restricted output.
- Promote development of worker to his maximum efficiency and prosperity.
- Ensure fair and reasonable division of work and responsibility between management and labour.

Taylor's observations on Scientific Management are really praiseworthy. Its significance lies on the emphasis he places on the use of the scientific method and the scientific approach for solving the management problems.

Henry Laurence Gantt

Being a contemporary and close associate of F.W. Taylor, Henry Laurence Gantt has given outstanding contribution to the development of scientific management. His contributions appeared in the many books and papers he wrote on management. *Works, Wages and Profits*[48], *Industrial Leadership*[49], *Organising for Work*[50] are the famous books in which Gantt expressed his management ideas. He also wrote many papers, which appeared in the many volumes of the newspaper of the 'American Society of Mechanical Engineers' (ASME) between 1902, and 1918. He developed graphic methods in designing and operating the techniques on managerial control. He pointed out the importance of time as well as cost in planning and controlling work. Among the many charts he designed 'Gantt Chart' is very famous which shows the amount of time needed to perform an activity. Managers use this chart to compare the actual work with that of the planned one. Since this chart helps to control the production it is also known as 'daily balance sheet chart.'

Frank Bunker Gilbreth and Mrs. Lillian Moller Gilbreth

Frank and Lillian Gilbreth, a team of husband and wife also strongly supported the ideas of F. W. Taylor on scientific management. The book, *Cheaper by the Dozen*[51], which, F.B. Gilbreth co-authored with E.G. Carey and *Time Out for Happiness*[52] authored by F.B. Gilbreth are important contributions to management studies. With a rare combination of talents Lillian Gilbreth's interest was in efficiency—the search for the one best way of doing a given task. There is no doubt that they succeeded in their effort. They spent their whole lives in their search for better work methods and put forward systematic rules and procedures for the efficient operation of work, and insisted that the workers should keep the same. In return, employees were given more than the competitor's rate. The employees had no other way except to accept the pre determined scientific process to do the job.

With this approach the function of planning was separated from doing. They discovered a micro –chronometer, a cycle graph, the chronocycle graph, the process chart and the flow diagram. The contributions of Gilbreths to the field of management are most admirable. In the words of Edwin H. Schell, "the greatest event of our time in the field of scientific management was the professional teaming up of the Gilbreths, in one of the strongest combinations of complimentary talents that we shall ever witness."[53]

Henri Fayol

Henri Fayol, a French Industrialist developed and applied scientific method to the problem of personnel and its management. His *book General and Industrial Administration*[54] is famous. This work is important because it was in this work that he developed a fully comprehensive definition of industrial management. He identified six activities of any industrial undertaking and named them: (1) technical; (2) commercial; (3) financial; (4) security; (5) accounting; and (6) managerial[55]. Fayol's primary focus, of course, was on this last managerial activity because he felt managerial skills had been the most neglected aspect of business operations. He defined management in terms of five significant functions: planning, organising, commanding, coordinating and controlling. He also listed 14 principles of management as general guides to the management process and management practice. He claimed that these principles are the foundation of his own success. These principles can be listed as follows:

Division of Work

The main purpose of division of work is to produce more and better work with the same effort. This is the specialisation, which ensures efficiency in the use of labour and this principle can be applied to all kinds of work, managerial as well as technical.

Authority and Responsibility

It clearly defines the rights and duties of managers and the performance expected of them. It defines the area of action, initiative and responsibility of each manager.

Discipline

This principle is the soul of teamwork and the basis of organised industry. It ensures obedience and respect for the agreements between the firm and its employees and sees that everybody receives the same standard of treatment in the firm.

Unity of Command

It provides the security against confusion. According to this principle each employee should have an identified and recognised superior or commander.

Unity of Direction

This principle ensures that there is only one commander for each activity or objective.

Subordination of Individual Interest to Group Interest or Organisational Interest

In an organisation an employee is always concerned with maximising his own satisfaction through more money, recognition, status etc. But the general interest of the company is always in favour of maximising the production. Fayol stresses that here an individual should forego his interest for the common good of the organisation.

Remuneration

The remuneration given to the employees should be fair and reasonable. They should consider the cost of living, productivity of the concerned employees, general business conditions and capacity of the firm while fixing the remuneration. Fair remuneration increases worker's efficiency and morale and brings about good relations with the management.

Centralisation and Decentralisation

If the organisation gives more power to subordinates in management, it is decentralisation and if they give less involvement to them, it is centralisation. The management should decide the degree of centralisations or decentralisation of authority on the basis of individual circumstances.

Scalar Chain

Scalar chain refers to the line of authority from the highest executive to the lowest for the purpose of communication. It governs superior-subordinate relationship and the authority of superiors in relation to subordinates at various levels.

Order

This relates to the arrangement of things and people. In material order, there should be a place for everything and everything should be in its place. Similarly, in social order, right man should be appointed in the right place.

Equity

The principle of equity ensures justice and fair dealings to subordinates from a manager. It requires managers to be free from all types of prejudices and personal likes or dislikes. This will create healthy industrial relations between management and labour, which is necessary for the successful functioning of the enterprise.

Stability of Job Tenure

It is a basic motivation for attention to work interest, and sustained efforts of the employees. This principle points out the dangers and costs of unnecessary turnover of employees.

Initiative

This encourages creative thinking and initiative on the part of everyone who works in the organisation. Fayol believes that initiative is one of the keenest satisfactions for an intelligent man to experience, and hence, he advises managers to give their employees maximum opportunity to express their ideas and show their initiative.

Esprit de corps

This is the principle of 'Union is strength' and stresses the need for teamwork. Only when all the personnel work together as a team there is scope for realising the objectives of the concern, and hence managers should encourage team spirit among the employees.

Both Taylor and Fayol had the same goal of increasing production, but they tried to reach this goal from different angles. Taylor worked from bottom of the hierarchy upward and Fayol from the top downwards. Writers on management and managers themselves accepted Fayol's principles wholeheartedly and drawing inspiration from Fayol, a new school of thought known as the *Management Process School* came into existence. Harold Koontz and Cyril O' Donnel are the founders of this school. They believe that management is a dynamic process, which performs the functions of planning, organising, staffing, directing and controlling. They also believe that these functions and the principles on which they are based have general or universal applicability and that management theory, as a body of knowledge, is not culture bound, but is transferable from one environment to another.

In the first stage of the history of management, which we termed the scientific era of management, there are mainly four contributors. In Winslow Taylor we have beginning of this era, which was followed further by Laurence Gantt, the Gilbreth and Henry Fayol. In Taylor the stress was on better production and achievement in the management field. He looked at the whole management process as an object to be organised and technically perfected. All the principles, which he gave, are meant for achieving this end. As we come to Gantt the stress is more on the management of time. That is to say for him two raw materials used in the management 'industry' are time – time of all the individuals involved in the process and cost – the money, area and things which are used in the process. The question was how these raw materials are made use of the maximum for the better profit issuing from them. The Gilbreths took management to a different stage. In fact, though the human approach is listed as the second stage in this dissertation it had shown its head in germinal form in the Gilbreth. Their insight into the process of management made them realise that the worker is very important and has to be given sufficient consideration. The problem with these two writers was that they separated planning from the actual doing.

Henry Fayol is closer to the next stage of the history of management. He also understands management as a system to be tackled by improving the different items involved in it. At the same time he was well aware of the human factor in this whole process. When he speaks of the division of work, unity of command, unity of direction etc he has in mind the fact that we are dealing with human being and therefore clarity and unity have to guide those involved in the management.

Thus in the first stage of management thought we learn that there has been a great effort from management thinkers to study the management process from different angles. They formulated scientific management principles and management functions generally applicable to organisations at different levels.

Second Stage—Emphasis on Human Relationship in Management

This stage is marked by the emphasis given to human relationship in the functioning of organisations and firms. Earlier, in the first stage the stress was on the non-human factors in management. These factors were closely observed and scientific conclusions were arrived at. But the human element in management was not given adequate importance. But in the second stage of management science what was left out or improperly studied in the first stage was given due importance. For the smooth functioning of organisations and the attainment of the desired results, it is found, that it is absolutely necessary that healthy relationship exists between the manager and the workers and among the workers themselves. Already in the pre scientific period of management study Robert Owen had brought to light the importance of human relationship. But he did not take his observations to scientific conclusions. But later in the second stage of the evolution of the science of management human relationship was given importance. In this period of development of the management science Elton Mayo and Roethelisberger, Mary Parker Follett, Dale Carnegie, Lawrence J. Peter, Max Weber, Hugo Munsterberg are the main contributors.

Elton Mayo and Roethlisberger

Elton Mayo was a consultant at Harvard University and Roethlisberger was his associate. They started with the practical application of Taylor's scientific techniques in management. Mayo is known in management field as the founder of the human relations movement in industry. His main work is *the Political Problem of an Industrial Society*.[56] His statement "economic theory in its human aspect is woefully inadequate; indeed it is absurd. Humanity is not adequately described as a horde of individuals, each activated by self-interest..."[57] is very famous.

He conducted experiments in four stages starting from 1927 and ending in 1936.[58] The first stage of his experiment was to evaluate the hypothesis that productivity and working conditions are directly proportionate. In other words, the hypothesis said that if the working conditions in a firm were improved there would be proportionate increase in productivity. To find out the truth of this hypothesis he conducted experiments at the Hawthorne Plant of the Western Electric Company in 1927. This is the first stage of a series of experiments. He improved the lighting system for a group of female workers in the company. The lighting system of another group was kept unchanged. But there was no marked difference in the productivity of these two groups. In other words the improvement in the lighting system did not improve productivity. On account of other factors the output of both the groups continued to improve. In the second stage the experiment was extended to the length and timing of the intervals. Here also one group was given different timing and length of interval, while another group had unchanged timings and length of intervals. Here also it was found that increase in the length of the break did not have effect on the output. In this stage of his experiment he had the interesting experience that some female workers complained that the interval time was too long and that they lost the rhythm of work. In the third stage of his experiment he made a survey of more than 20000 employees. He wanted to know the attitudinal changes in the employees. Here also the hypothesis that improved working conditions guaranteed proportionate increase in output was proved false. The fourth stage of his experiments concentrated on observing the formal and informal working groups. From these experiments he came to the conclusion that unless the workers felt the "communal responsibility" and that "they belonged to the new social group" the output cannot be increased.[59] He also observed that as the workers feel a communal responsibility and sense of belongingness their complaints also decline.

From the experiences he gained from these four stages of experiments, Mayo came to the conclusion that "interaction, companionship and contribution to common purpose"[60] are the decisive factors in the functioning of a firm or an organisation. As a result, he started personal counselling schemes to improve the relationship between the manager and the employees and among the employees themselves. These series of experiments are known as the Hawthorne studies. The main two contributions of these studies are: (1) human relationship; and (2) social man.

Mary Parker Follett

The contribution of Mary Parker Follett to management studies is that she also shifted the interest from the non-human factors to the human factors in the organisations. She expressed her insights in the books and papers she wrote from 1909 to 1949.[61] "She believed that groups were the mechanisms through which people could combine their differing talents for the greater good of the organisation which she defined as 'community' in which managers and subordinates could work in harmony".[62] She is famous for her insights into group psychology and group dynamics. Unless the group psychology of the workers is properly tapped a manger cannot function successfully. She said "instead of preparing and training managers to give orders they should be trained to work with employees so that they can together attain the organisational goals."[63]

We can identify four principles which emerged as a result of her research.[64] The first one refers to the relationship between the manager and workers. This relationship should have a personal and human touch. The second one is the participative basis of cooperation in the organisation. That is to say, the employees should feel that they have a participative role in the whole affair of the firm. The third principle concerns cooperation. In the firm there should be the atmosphere of cooperation. Every one should feel that they are cooperating with each other for the common good. So it is a matter of faith and this faith should be maintained for the smooth functioning of the firm. The fourth principle points to reciprocity or mutuality. That is to say, the cooperation from the part of the workers and their generosity and enthusiasm should be properly reciprocated from the part of the authorities.

Dale Carnegie

Carnegie's contribution also was on the lines of improving human relationship in the firms and organisations. He was faced with the problem of non-profitable and ineffective activities and solved these problems by suggesting the method of what he called "overcoming fears". The main factor in improving human relationship is empathy, that is to say, "the ability to put yourselves in the other person's position seeing things from their point of view, understanding their wants, needs, hope and fears; understanding what they want from the transaction…"[65] Many are the suggestions put forward by Carnegie. He insisted that the customers have a right to feel important and to have their needs satisfied: a genuine interest in people has to be developed. The language used in communications should be positive. Criticisms, though necessary at times, should be directed towards the mistakes they have committed and never towards their personality. When a wrongdoing is criticised, it should be complemented with positive suggestion for improvement. Of all the contributions of Carnegie, the most important is the central position he gives to the customer.[66]

Lawrence J. Peter

Another contribution to the human relationship stress on management came from Lawrence J. Peter. He is famous for the so-called Peter Principle.[67] He brought to light the illogicality with which promotions are given in traditional organisations. If a person is found to be successful in a particular level of the organisation, he or she is promoted to a higher level without considering whether the person has competency in the new level of action. Moreover, " More generally, what is ' sound performance' in one job may simply be identified on the basis that the individual is not actually doing any harm".[68]

In the second stage of the history of management we can see both similarities and dissimilarities in the different contributions of management thinkers. The common factor, perhaps, is that all of them were concerned about the human factor in the of management process. The satisfaction of the worker and his mental health are important factors, which contribute to the better performance in the factories and the firms. Therefore better working conditions are to be ensured and salary, proportionate to the needs of the workers is to be given. Salary should not only be proportionate to the output but also proportionate to the needs of the workers. In promotion every factor that contributed to the successful management of a particular employee is to be taken to consideration. This means those in authority should not be easily taken away by first impressions. Here the Peter Principle is very significant. As a whole in this stage the stress is on the human element in management. The human element means that in the management process as there are things there are also persons. The second factor is much more important than the first. The stress is on the second factor, the human factor or the person-factor. Only when sufficient thought is given to the second factor, management can bring the desired success.

Third Stage—Social Sciences and Management

This stage is both a continuation of the second stage namely the human relationship era and an improvement upon it. In this era of management studies the insights gained from social sciences, behavioural sciences and psychology and sciences related to them were put together to gain more information about the way an organisation functions. Social scientists and Organisation theorists had a common belief that best result can be expected by developing theories of management and organisation based on the findings of the behavioural scicnces such as psychology, sociology psychiatry, economics, cultural anthropology and philosophy. Emphasis is given to the behavioural pattern of individuals. This period is specially noted for the development of human behaviour school and social system school.

Major findings of this stage are that human element is the key factor in the success or failure of an organisation and that people like to be consulted rather than receive orders or information. The main contributors to this stage of management studies are Douglas McGregor, L.F. Urwick, William Ouchi, Abraham Maslow, Chris Argyris, Chester Bernard, Rensis Likert, and Frederick Herzberg.

Douglas McGregor, L.F. Urwick and William Ouchi: X, Y, and Z Theories

In the social sciences era of management studies, the contributions of McGregor and Urwick are epoch making. McGregor considered the traditional approach to management as the X theory. This is an authoritarian type of management and is dominated by the presuppositions like: (1) an average human being has an inherent dislike for work; (2) because of this human nature people have to be forced to work with directions, threatening, controlling and so on; (3) the average human beings avoid responsibility for himself or herself and want to be directed by others.

For McGregor, the X theory of management is the traditional or the scientific management theory with all the above presuppositions. In place of the X theory he proposed his new theory known as theory Y that was formulated in his many writings.[69] According to his findings, he said: (1) humans have a natural liking for exerting physical and mental effort in work. This is something like using his or her mental or physical powers for play and rest; (2) It is not only through external control and threat that humans can be directed to bring about the objectives. They also have the power to exercise self-control and self-direction. But this they will do only if they are committed to the objectives. Their commitment depends on the rewards expected or offered; (3) Human beings have the innate nature to seek responsibility and not only to be directed by others.[70]

Improving upon the Y theory of McGregor, another management thinker by name Urwick proposed his theory known as theory Z.[71] He distinguishes between man as consumer and man as producer or distributor. The success of an enterprise depends on bridging the gap between man as consumer and man as distributor or producer. The leadership in a firm should see that this gap is bridged. According to him the reason for the failures in the running of the firms is that the workers are not aware of the common purpose. To make them aware is basic for success. The communication between the consumer and producer or distributor is very often imperfect. When this imperfection is removed, there will be successful functioning in the organisation.

Though Urwick proposed his theory as a new theory with a new name, it is doubtful whether he has proposed a new one. In fact his views are almost identical with the ideas of McGregor. In the Y theory all these insights were already expressed. Urwick's contribution is to be seen perhaps, in the new way in which he proposed the Y theory by the name of theory Z.

William Ouchi is another researcher who proposed a new theory for efficiency and greater productivity in organisations. As Urwick proposed theory Z Ouchi also proposed a theory by the same name namely theory Z. Though the name is the same the context from which they came to the theory and the suggestions made in the theory are widely different. Ouchi received inspirations from the functioning of Japanese firms and companies. Aiming at improving upon McGregor's theory Y, Ouchi proposed theory Z as a new situation to the problems faced by managers. The situation in Japanese companies is entirely different from that in European companies. In the Japanese companies "the firms needed to provide a paternalistic treatment of employees to supplant the social patterns of feudalism."[72] The companies provided for all the needs of the employees so much so that the employees felt committed to the cause of the companies. Even the not very competent people were taken care of. The employees were transferred in such a way that they got experience in diverse functions. There is much discussion and sharing of information. The focus is on the group and not on the individuals. The whole person of the employee is accepted and not simply his particular technical skill. This resulted in

> Employee satisfaction and sense of autonomy, the later being experienced by yielding a kind of self-centred individualism to commitment to group and the transcendent company cause which, it is argued, can produce an even stronger sense of autonomy than that produced by more individualistic way so much vaunted in the West.[73]

Ouchi suggested that this atmosphere should exist in the company and he named it theory Z.

Theory Z of William Ouchi has its merits especially as it wants to create a more cordial atmosphere within the firm. Cordiality will be ethically more desirable than a situation of autocracy. But on two points Ouchi's theory Z has been criticised by other researchers and writers. The first problem with this theory is that its presuppositions about Japanese companies are not founded on evidence. It is true that there are some Japanese companies where the above situations exist but not in all. The fact is that in some Japanese companies autocracy and beaurocracy exist as much as in Western companies. The second problem with this theory is that it is not proved beyond doubt whether the cordial atmosphere in the company will necessarily improve productivity.

Abraham Maslow

The theory based on human needs proposed by Abraham Maslow is another contribution to the social science period of management studies. Man has mainly two needs—physiological needs and psychological needs. Under these there are many sub needs. Altogether Maslow has found out five basic needs of man. The first is the physiological needs for the maintenance of the person. Food, water etc are the needs of this type. The second need is safety. Man needs safety such as security, protection, stability etc. Then comes the third need, which is social need. The longing for love, affection, sense of belongingness etc are to be included in the social need. The next in the ladder is esteem need under which the desires for respect, prestige, recognition, self-esteem etc are included. The highest position is enjoyed by self-actualisation need. That is, the need to grow and bring to full maturity all the creative talents of man. Since the needs are felt in the order of hierarchy starting from the physiological and ending with the self-actualisation, humans will long for the fulfilment of the next higher need when one of his needs is fulfilled. According to Maslow the problem with many of the firms and organisations is that they don't approach the workers with this need consciousness. A manager will do all the things for fulfilling the physical needs. The workers are satisfied. But next they will be longing for the next need with the result that they will not put up effectiveness in work unless that need is met. But many managers go on satisfying the same need over and over again without a thought for the higher needs for the fulfilment of which the workers are yearning.

Chris Argyris

In the social sciences period of management studies the contributions of Chris Argyris are worth mentioning. His theory known as the Immaturity-Maturity theory is famous. He started with the oft-repeated complaint by managers that the employees are lazy people. But Chris Argyris, through his studies and researches, came to the conclusion that laziness was not the reason for employee apathy rather the fact was that they were often treated like little children. His immaturity- maturity theory is based on this finding.

In this theory Argyris explained the different stages of growth of human personality, which ultimately will take him to the level of a fully matured person. The journey from immaturity to maturity is a long process in which a number of key changes take place. Argyris points out the main signs of an immature worker in a firm or organisation. He may be a passive observer; needing the support and help for everything he does; having no plan of his own or interest in the work etc. But when he starts to grow to maturity he becomes more active with independent views and opinions about the organisation and it's working with wide circle of relationship. He becomes a person with deep interest and commitment to organisation and so on. According to Argyris though in the beginning each individual may not be a fully matured person he/she will become a matured one in the long process of their career life. He states that the organisation which sees individuals as immature persons expect them to be passive, dependant and subordinate, i.e. they are expected to behave immaturely. If in this way, an organisation treats individuals who are relatively mature it will lead them to the state of frustration and discontentment. This will finally force them to create some informal organisations wherein they can feel free and behave like matured persons. Such persons may turn against the formal hierarchy and oppose the common interest of the organisation.

This theory reveals some basic truths, which the managers of organisations are to practise. They should accept that each individual is unique and they are mature in their own field and can take wise decisions and behave intelligently. The manager has to understand the human needs and their desires and be tactful enough to integrate their needs with that of the needs of the organisation. If the manager succeeds in this venture it will result in more co-operation and commitment from the part of the workers for the realisation of the goals of the organisation.

Chester I. Bernard

Chester I. Bernard is another main contributor to management studies in this stage. He published a book entitled *The Functions of the Executive*[74] in the year 1938. This work is considered as the most influential book on management studies. Being a lifelong executive and president of the New Jersey Bill Telephone Company from 1927 to 1948, Bernard was a great scholar and intellectual. He was greatly influenced by Mayo and other faculty members at Harvard University, where he was an occasional lecturer. In his opinion, an organisation exists when the following three essential conditions are fulfilled:

(*a*) there are persons able to communicate with each other;

(*b*) they are willing to contribute to group action;

(*c*) they are ready to accomplish a common purpose.

The major contributions of Bernard directly concern the concept and constituents of organisation. The main points can be listed as follows:

Concept of Organisation

For explaining the concept of organisation he has defined it as a "system of consciously co-ordinated activities or courses of two or more persons".

Classification of Organisation

He classified organisations into formal and informal. The formal organisation has consciously co-ordinated interactions among persons, which have a deliberate, and a common objective. The informal organisation on the other hand, has social interactions, which do not have such common and co-ordinated purpose. In fact the main objective of informal organisation is to overcome the problems of formal organisation. So he suggested that executives should encourage the growth of informal organisation.

Elements of Organisation

According to Bernard the incentives of status, power, good physical conditions, opportunities of participation and good social conditions are the important elements of organisation. He argues that material reward is of crucial significance only up to a definite point.

Authority

Bernard has given a new concept of authority, which is termed as 'acceptance theory of authority' or 'bottom-up authority', and he is vehemently against the idea of top-down authority. He believes that a person will accept a communication as being authoritative only when four conditions are met simultaneously: The four conditions are: "(*a*) he can and thus understands the communication; (*b*) at the time of his decision he believes that it is not inconsistent with the purpose of the organisation; *(c)* at the time of his decision he believes it to be compatible with his personal interest as a whole; and *(d)* he is able mentally and physically to comply with it."[75]

Functions of Executive

In the words of Bernard the executive work is "the specialised work of maintaining the organisation in operation". This demands three basic tasks on the part of the executive:

(a) the maintenance of organisational communication;

(b) the securing of essential services from individuals; and

(c) the formulation of purpose and objective.

Motivation

In his opinion different persons are motivated at different times at different types of incentives. He gave more importance to factors like opportunity of distinction and power, pride of workmanship, pleasant organisations, participation, mutual supporting personal attitudes, and the feeling of belongingness.

Executive Leadership

The essence of executive leadership is the "creative function" of the executive. Executive leadership demands high calibre, technological competence, technical and social skills. The executive leadership should not have pre-conceived notions and false ideologies.

Organisational Equilibrium

Organisational Equilibrium is the matching of individual efforts and organisational efforts to satisfy individuals. His concept of equilibrium is not static. It depends on the individuals, organisation, and society.

The above contributions of Bernard show how he was concerned for the development of the organisation through social systems. He was so brilliant and realistic in analysing the work of organisation.

Rensis Likert

Among the behavioural scientists Rensis Likert is one of the most famous. He was a psychologist as well as a sociologist. His books, *"New Patterns of Management"*[76] and *"The Human Organisation"* brought him to the forefront of researchers and thinkers in the field of management. He has suggested four systems of management. *System 1* management is called "exploitative-authoritative"; such managers are highly autocratic and have no confidence or trust in subordinates. They motivate people through threats and punishment with occasional rewards. They believe in downward communication, and limit decision making to the top. *System 2* management is described as "benevolent-authoritative". These managers have some patronising confidence and trust in subordinates just as a master has in his servant. He motivates the workers with rewards and some threat and punishment. He also permits some upward communication etc. *System 3* management is known as "consultative", these managers have substantial but not complete confidence and trust in the subordinates, and therefore, the management consults them sometimes and encourage teamwork. *System 4* management is referred to as "participative", these managers have complete trust and confidence in the subordinates in all matters, always receive ideas and suggestions from subordinates and constructively use them, give economic rewards on the basis of group participation and involvement in particular areas, involve in communication down and up etc.[77]

Likert strongly recommends the participative form of management. He believes that "of all the tasks of management, managing the human component is the central and most important task, because all else depends upon how well it is done." Likert is also well known for developing his famous 'Linking Pin Model' of organisation, which is based on the idea that every individual in the organisation is an important member of two groups. An individual acts in an organisation as a linking pin for the units in the organisation above and below him. The individual is a group leader of the lower unit and a group member of the upper unit. The focus is upward and a group-to-group relationship exists in this model instead of man-to-man relationship. This upward focus to the organisation is found in the achievement of goals, communication, supervisory influence etc. Later on he modified this model and added horizontal linkage to the model.

Frederick Herzberg

As an extension and application of Maslow's need hierarchy concept Frederick Herzberg has made a substantial contribution to work motivation. According to him job satisfaction was related to "job content" and job dissatisfaction was associated with 'job context'. The factors, which give "satisfaction" are termed as 'motivators' and those which give "dissatisfaction" as 'hygiene factors'.

Hygiene factors are those factors the absence of which brings about dissatisfaction and the presence of which do not motivate workers to greater productivity and efficiency but only prevent the performance of a work from coming down; it includes company policies and administration, supervision, working conditions, inter-personal relations, salary, status and security. The motivators are positive factors, or satisfiers, which contribute to positive, effect and result in higher productivity and efficiency. It covers achievement, recognition, responsibility, advancement and growth. Since the theory explains the relative effect of two factors on motivation of workers, it is known as the *'Two-Factor Theory of Motivation'* or *Motivation-Hygiene Theory*.[78]

Other Contributors to the Study of Management in the Third Stage

When management study took over ideas and ideals from other sciences the contributions of behavioural sciences were found to be most nourishing and effective. Among the behavioural scientists the names of Homans, Bakke, Lewin, Katz, and Khan are very important. All these people concentrated their attention on the behaviour of individuals individually and in-group. Their findings were found to be most helpful for the effective running of the firms and organisations.

Homans[79] speak of three basic elements of group-interaction, activity and sentiment. Any group when it is formed into a group acts in this way. Interaction is a term that refers to the inter-personal behaviour of the individuals within the group. In interaction speech is not important. For example true tennis players are interacting. But they may not be speaking with each other. The pattern of interaction varies from group to group. For example in a class room there is interaction between the teacher and the students. If the teacher is initiating the teaching and monopolising interaction the involvement of others is minimum. But there is interaction. Activity is the next element in group-behaviour. Activity is the thing that people do in a group-walking, sitting, eating etc. The pattern of activities also differs from group to group. Sentiment is the other element. It "includes those emotional and mental processes that are inside people and cannot be seen but whose presence is inferred from people's activities and interactions."[80] Smile is an activity. But it suggests a particular sentiment. There are different sentiments shown by various such activities.

These three elements of group-behaviour are interdependent. It is, in fact the interdependence of these three elements of group behaviour, which help us in properly managing an organisation. Very often activity and interaction are considered together as behaviour. So behaviour and sentiment are interlinked. A change in behaviour is very often a sign that there is change in sentiment. But it is always not the case. Sometimes a particular behaviour follows a particular sentiment. Some other times the sentiments follow the behaviour. Whatever be the sequence interdependence is clear. So this knowledge will help the manager to handle the situation in a positive way.

The contribution of Daniel Katz and Robert Khan[81] is known as in-organisation motivation model. They proposed four in-organisation motive patterns. They are: (1) authority and discipline; (2) demanding job content; (3) systemic reward of good work; (4) matching individual needs and goals. If there is proper authority and discipline there will be healthy atmosphere in a firm. That is what is meant by the first motive pattern. But the authority has to be "exercised with fairness" and then "it creates a healthy atmosphere in the enterprise against a non-performing, gossiping crowd corrupting the air of natural motivation."[82] The workers should be convinced that a minimum of performance is sine qua non condition for survival in the firm. They should also know that authority is exercised fairly. The second motive pattern namely demanding job content refers to the situation in which "the jobs are set and enriched in such a way as to draw the best result and resourcefulness from the employees."[83] The third motive pattern refers to the rewarding for good performance. It includes many things. (1) First of all there should be opportunity for good work; (2) Then there should be people for identifying good work; and (3) finally good work should be proportionately rewarded. The fourth motive pattern may be explained as follows: The individual employee has his or her own private goals. Then there is the common goal for the firm or organisation. These two goals should conform to each other. The employees should feel that their own goal is identified with the goal of the organisation. This will create a feeling of fulfilment.

The contribution of Kurt Lewin is in the direction of organisational change. There are two types of organisational change: one is planned and other is unplanned. Unplanned change is a partial reaction to the events that occur in the environment. Since it is unplanned it has the danger of ineffectiveness in the firm. Planned change is implemented in an orderly way by anticipating the future events. Lewin says that a three-stage process is to be followed in introducing the planned change. The three stages are: (1) unfreezing; (2) changing; (3) refreezing. By unfreezing he means creating a felt need for the change. The manager should meet all the people concerned and make them understand that the present situation is ineffective and a change is needed. The second stage namely changing refers to the actual change that is implemented. But the managers have to be extremely careful in this stage. They have to identify the more effective behaviours to be followed. They also have to have clear ideas about the new tasks, people, technology and so on. Refreezing, the third stage of planned change, refers to the stabilisation of the change. The manager has to "create an acceptance and continuity for the new behaviours" and "provide the required resources support for the change."[84]

Improving upon Kurt Lewin's planned organisational change model Moorhead and Griffin[85] came out with what is called expanded change process model. They found that Lewin's model fails to take into account certain "critical dimensions of the change situation".[86] According to expanded change process model there are altogether six stages or processes. First the top management recognises the forces leading to a change. Then he recognises and defines the problem. Then there is a process of solving the problem and this results in the implementation of the change. While the change is implemented the change is measured, evaluated and controlled and the transition is properly managed. In this process steps 2, 3, 4 and 5 are considered together as the change agent.

The third stage in the history of management study is a follow up from the second stage. This was an era of great contributions in human sciences like psychology, sociology, social psychology and so on. Comparing the second and the third stages we can say what is special about the third stage is that it combines the human, the group and process factors together in evaluating and suggesting improvement in the management of companies and firms. The workers are first and foromost human persons. Therefore the human factor is important. But they are not to be considered simply as individuals because they function as a group. Therefore, the group psychology has to have a say in evaluating their performance. Thirdly they function in a process. In other words what they do is not simply repetition of the very same things, but also a process of growth from one stage to another. For example in a factory, which produces car, the workers stationed in every part of the company have only to repeat the very same products. Those making the wheels go on repeating the same thing. Those who make the steering also repeat the same thing. At the same time what comes out of the factory is not simply a huge number of wheels and steering, but cars. That means the work is a process. Unless this process factor is taken into serious consideration there is always the danger of fatigue and tiredness produced by the repetition of the work. So the contribution of the third stage is that the different factors are taken into serious consideration.

Thus in the third stage of management history behavioural scientists have contributed a lot both for the development of workers and to the organisation as a whole. The central point of this stage is that if a manager succeeds in utilising the human resources to its maximum he can expect better performance from workers in the development of organisation. The more we can understand human needs, the more it will be possible to integrate them with the needs of organisations.

Fourth Stage—Management as a Science by Itself

In the fourth stage we can see a great move on the part of economists and mathematicians to prove that management is a science by itself. The writers and researchers who contributed for the development of management into the fourth stage wanted to reduce management to certain theories, which they claimed to belong particularly, and to some extent even exclusively to management itself. Here the trend is not to depend on other sciences and receive insights from them; rather to develop theories and principles applicable to management itself. In this stage we can identify at least two schools, which have contributed for looking at management as a science by itself. These two schools are decision-making school and mathematical school.

The decision theory school looks at management as a series of decision-making. Most of the members of the school are economic theorists. Decision itself is a course of action to be followed in a given situation and it refers to the selection from among possible alternatives of a course of actions. Decision always presupposes different alternatives. If there is only one way of doing a thing it is a sign that that one way is the wrong way. If we are able to think of only one way of doing a thing that is also a sign that we have not given a serious thought to that particular matter. Therefore decision-making presupposes the existence of many alternatives, i.e., the manager has to develop different alternatives. "The ability to develop alternatives is often as important as selecting correctly from among them."[87] Choosing the correct course of action from among the different alternatives is decision making. The more rational the decision-making is the better the result will be. In the process of making the decision G.A. Cole identifies seven steps. First is to define the problem or the issue at hand. The second one is to collect the relevant data. The next step is to develop alternative solutions to the problem. Fourthly one has to assess the consequences of the particular solution suggested. In the next step one selects the optimum (the best) solution. Then one moves to implement the solution. And finally the results are measured. In decision-making school of management, "the theory of satisficing" of Herbert Simon is very famous. Theory of satisficing says that since we are not able to come to the most intelligent decision what is possible is only a decision or a course of action "that is satisfactory or good enough under the circumstances."[88]

Another School of thought in the fourth stage of the evolution of management is the so-called *mathematical school* also known as *quantitative measurement school*. J.W.Forrester[89], Stafford Beer[90], R.L.Ackoff[91] are some of the main contributors to the studies in mathematical approach to management. The school presents management primarily as a mathematical process with concepts, symbols and models. It sees management as a system of mathematical models and therefore it is closely related to the other school namely the decision theory school. This school of thought is based on the idea that "if management involves a rational and logical pattern, the pattern can best be expressed through the use of mathematics, which is also logically based."[92] Thus the foundation of mathematical school is the decision theory school and it applies "statistics in decision making and the evolution of mathematical/econometric model that are nurtured by computer technology."[93] Here we can identify four characteristics of the school. (1) The Primary focus of the school is decision making; (2) It is based on economic decision theory; (3) It uses formal mathematical model; (4) There will be the extensive use of computers.

This approach is applied mainly in three fields-management science fields, operations management field and management information systems field. Management science is not the same as scientific management of Taylor. It is a modern approach to management, which "involves the use of highly sophisticated techniques, statistical tools and complex models."[94]

Operations management is concerned with the tasks of production and the control of the operations. For this mathematics is not extensively used. Yet for forecasting inventory control, linear programming, queuing theory, network, break-even analysis, simulation, regression analysis etc mathematical approach is used. Another field in which mathematical approach is used is management information system, which is very often expressed in abbreviation as MIS. The MIS networks are mostly computerised because of the complexity involved.

In short the mathematical approach is very widely used with it the decision making approach also. "The mathematical school is developing fast. The use of mathematics and different quantitative techniques is increasing. The use of this technique has added respectability to the discipline of management and it has brought an element of exactness in management, which is a social science."[95] Yet this school cannot be taken as a flawless school. Though mathematics has contributed much to management, management cannot be reduced to mathematics because, as R.N. Singh says, "it can only be treated as a tool in managerial practice."[96]

Fifth Stage—Integrated Management Thought (*Present Stage*)

In modern times no theory is blindly accepted as suitable for solving problems in management. This is not to deny the merits of these theories. Rather it is based on the awareness of the limitations of these theories. Each method has its own merits and demerits. Therefore the best approach would be to take the best of everything and leave the negative aspects. The integrated management thought accommodates the best of each approach. In modern times integrated management thought has found expression in two theories-Contingency theory and Systems Theory.

Contingency Theory

Contingency theory is based on the supposition that proper management technique in a given situation cannot be stated in advance, since the nature and type of management problem varies always. Methods and techniques highly effective in one situation may not find success in some other situation. According to contingency approach it is the duty of task manager to identify the proper technique suitable in a particular situation.[97] So managers must possess a kind of situational sensitivity and practical selectivity.

Contingency approach is suitable in designing organisational structure, in deciding the degree of decentralisation, in motivational and leadership approaches, in employee development and training programmes, in planning, controlling and communication system etc.

Systems Theory

The systems approach also provides an integrated approach to management problems. A system is a set of inter-related parts, which together form a whole unit that performs some functions. An organisation is considered as a system with a number of sub-systems like finance, accounting, marketing and production departments directed to some specific purpose. It is the manager who integrates the available facilities to achieve the goal. The sub-systems serve as the media through which the manager operates. Systems thinking helps to understand that a change made in one system can affect all the sub-systems. For example a change in production strategy could impact sales, distribution, advertising, pricing and finance. Synergy is expected to accrue when the manager effectively co-ordinates the efforts of related sub-systems. To be more precise if a manager is very efficient in coordinating the sub-systems the result will be higher than the sum total of similar independent efforts. To the mathematicians synergy is secured when 1+1 is greater than 2. To the efficiency expert, synergy is obtained when two employees, working together on a task, can do more work than two employees working independently. Thus systems approach also helps the manager to understand the inter-relatedness of each element in the organisation and to act accordingly.[98] We will speak more about the integrated management thought applied in modern times in the next chapter where we analyse the merits and demerits of each approach.

Conclusions

This short survey of the history of management thought and its development through different stages has made it clear that the subject is ever growing with the influence of many experts and thinkers in the field of behavioural sciences, psychology, etc. Each of these sciences has made its own particular contribution to the whole, but none has provided a comprehensive coverage of the field.

This study brought to light that management direction and leadership are separate from the functions, operations and activities of the organisation. Ability to create confidence, loyalty, trust and faith of all those in the organisation is the cornerstone for the overall realisation of the goal. People must be rewarded in response to the efforts that they put for the realisation of the organisation's purpose and the rewards should be not only in the form of money, but it should take other forms also. Managers must have enough knowledge, ability and wisdom to adopt an integrated approach to solve the management problems in an organisation in different situations.

REFERENCES

1. Adebowale Akande, "Human Resources Strategy: Focusing on Joseph's Analytic Work", *Management Decision*, MCB UP Ltd, Vol: 29, No: 7, 1991.

2. Braam Oberholster, "Management – A Christian Perspective"- Prepared for the International Faith and Learning Seminar held at Helderberg College, Somerset West, South Africa, Dec. 1993.

3. Donald W. McCormick, "Spirituality and Management", *Journal of Managerial Psychology*, Vol. 9, No. 6, 1994, pp. 5-8).
4. Laurie Beth Jones, Jesus CEO: *Using Ancient Wisdom for Visionary Leadership*, New York, Hyperion, 1995.
5. Laurie Beth Jones, *Jesus Entrepreneur*, New York, Three Rivers Press, 2001.
6. Anthony Scaperlanda, "John Paul II's Vision of the Role of Multinational Enterprise Expansion in Building the Social Economy", *International Journal of Social Economics*, Vol. 25, No. 11/12, MCB University Press, USA, 1998, pp. 1764-1775.
7. Rick L. Edgeman, "Training and Development: Principle Centered Leadership and Core Value Deployment" *The TQM Magazine*, Vol. 10, No: 3, MCB University Press, ISSN, 1998, pp. 190-193.
8. Michael Henry Kennedy, "Fayol's Principles and the Rule of St. Benedict: Is There Anything New Under the Sun?", *Journal of Management History*, Vol. 5, No. 5, Nova Southern University, Fort Lauderdale, Florida, USA, 1999, pp. 269-276
9. Low Sui Pheng, "Towards Managerial Efficacy: Back to 2000-year-old Guiding Principles", *The Learning Organisation*, Vol. 6, No. 3, MCB University Press, ISSN, 1999, pp. 121-131.
10. Rabbi Baron, *Moses on Management: 50 Leadership Lessons form the Greatest Manager of All Time*, Simon & Schuster, Adult Publishing Group, 2000 (w.w.w.amazon.com)
11. N.M. Khandelwal, *Management Concepts from the Mahabharata*, Delhi, New Century Publications, 2001.
12. Anthony A. D'Souza, *Leaders for Today Hope for Tomorrow*, Mumbai, Pauline Publications, 2001
13. Easo John, *A Christian Perspectives on Management*, Chennai, Dr. Easo John Associates, 2003
14. A. Gregory Stone, Robert F. Russel and Kathleen Patterson, Transformational Versus Servant Leadership: a Difference in Leader Focus", *The Leadership and Organisation Development Journal*, Vol. 25, No. 4, Emerald Group Publishing Limited, 2004, pp. 349-361
15. Lorin Woolfe, *The Bible on Leadership*, 2005 (http:// w.w.w.leadwell.com.)
16. J.S. Chandan, *Management Concepts and Strategies*, New Delhi, Vikas Publishing House Pvt. Ltd., 1997, p. 27.
17. R.J. Nogar, "Evolution Organic", *New Catholic Encyclopaedia*, Vol. 5, p. 692, 1967.

18. V.P. Michael, *Perspective Management*, Delhi, Himalaya Publishing House, 1994, p. 20.

19. This Distinction of Management and Administration of G. Milward is taken from T. Ramasamy, *Principles of Management*, New Delhi, Himalaya Publishing House, 2003, p. 18.

20. Cf. T. Ramasamy, *Principles of Management*, op. cit., pp. 16-20.

21. V.P. Michael, *Perspective Management*, op. cit., p. 21.

22. Ibid.

23. J.H. Donnelly, J.L. Gibson and J.M. Ivancevich, *Fundamentals of Management*, Massachusetts, Irwin McGraw-Hill, 1998, p. 5.

24. Cf. Adam Smith, An Enquiry in to the Nature and Causes of Wealth of the Nations, London, A. Strahan and T. Cadell, 1793.

25. Cf. J.S. Mill, *Principles of Political Economy*, (ed) Sir W.J. Ashley, London, Longmans, 1826.

26. J. Mill, *Elements of Political Economy*, London, Baldwin Cradock and Joy, 1826.

27. J.B. Say, *Catechism of Political Economy*, London, Sherwood, 1816.

28. Samuel P. Newman, *Elements of Political Economy*, Andover, Gould and Newman, 1835.

29. W.S. Jevons, *The Theory of Political Economy*, New York, The McMillan Company, 1888.

30. Robert Owen, *Socialism: A Primary Source Analysis*, Amazon, The Rosen Publishing Group, 1858

31. Charles Babbage, *On the Economy of Machinery and Manufacturers*, London, Charles Knight, 1832

32. H.R. Towne, "The Engineer as an Economist", Paper presented at the Conference of American Society of Mechanical Engineers, 1886.

33. J.S. Chandan, Management Concepts and Strategies, op. cit., p. 30.

34. J.S. Chandan, *Management Concepts and Strategies*, op. cit., pp. 30-31

35. R.N. Singh, *Management Thought and Thinkers*, New Delhi, Sultan Chand and Sons, 1977, p. 65

36. L.M. Prasad, *Principles and Practice of Management*, New Delhi, Sultan Chand and Sons, 2001, p. 4.

37. H. Koontz and H. Weihrich, *Management*, New York, McGraw-Hill Book Company, 1988, p. 9.

38. Babcock G.D, *The Taylor System in Franklin's Management*, New York, Engineering Magazine Company, 1927.

39. J.A.H. Murray and Other, *The Oxford English Dictionary*, Vol. 1, Oxford, Clarendon Press, 1978, p. 467.

40. G.R. Terry and S.G. Franklin, *Principles of Management*, Delhi, All India Traveller Book Seller, 1991.

41. R.N. Singh, *Management Thought and Thinkers*, op. cit., p. 22

42. G.R. Terry and S.G. Franklin, *Principles of Management*, op. cit., pp. 6-7.

43. All the Three Books are Combined in One Volume Entitled *Scientific Management,* New York, Harper & Row, 1947

44. Cf. Richard Pettinger, *Introduction to Management*, New York, Palgrave, 2002, p. 13.

45. F.W. Taylor, *Principles of Scientific Management*, New York, Harper, 1911 as Quoted by Gene Burton and M. Thakur op. cit., p. 39.

46. Cf. J.C. Sinha and V.N. Mugali, *Business Management*, New Delhi, R.C. Chand and Company, 1977. p. 36.

47. F.W. Taylor, *Principles of Scientific Management*, New York, Harper & Brothers, 1947, p. 37 as quoted by R.N. Singh, *Management Thought and Thinkers*, Delhi, Sultan Chand and Sons, p. 76. It seems the Quotation is not Correct. The Original Word would be *Contention* in the Place of *Contentment*.

48. H.L. Gantt, *Works Wages and Profits*, New York, Engineering Magazine Col, 1910.

49. H.L. Gantt, *Industrial Leadership*, New Haven, Yale University Press, 1916.

50. H.L. Gantt, *Organising for Work*, New York, Har Court Brace and Howe, 1919.

51. F.B. Gilbreth Jr and E.G. Carey, *Cheaper by the Dozen*, New York, Thomas Y Crowell, 1971.

52. F.B. Gilbreth Jr, *Time Out for Happiness*, New York, Thomas Y Crowell, 1971.

53. R.N. Singh, *Management Thought and Thinkers*, op. cit., p. 85.

54. Henri Fayol, *General and Industrial Administration*, New York, Pitman Publishing Corporation 1949.

55. Cf. R. Pettinger, Introduction to Management, op. cit., p. 12.

56. E. Mayo, *The Political Problem of an Industrial Society*, Cambridge, Harvard University, 1947.

57. E. Mayo, The Political Problem of an Industrial Society, op. cit., p. 21.

58. H. Koontz and H. Weihrich, *Management*, op. cit., p. 35.

59. Cf. D.R. Hampton, *Management*, (3rd edition), New York, McGraw-Hill Book Company, 1987, p. 52.

60. Ibid.

61. The main books are: 1) *The Speaker of the Use of Representative*, New York, Longman, 1909; 2) *The New State*, New York, Longman, 1920; 3) *Creative Experience*, New York, Longman, 1924; 4) *Business Management As a Profession*, (ed) H.C. Metcalf, Chicago, A. W. Shaw and Company, 1927; 5) *Dynamic Administration: The Collected Papers of Mary Parker Follett, (ed)* M. Metcalf and L. Urwick, London, Pitman, 1941; (6) *Freedom and Coordination: Lectures in Business Organisation* by Mary Parker Follett, (ed) L. Urwick, London, Pitman, 1949.

62. G. Burton, and M. Thakur, *Management Today: Principles and Practice*, op. cit., p. 48.

63. J.S. Chandan, Management Concepts and Strategies, op. cit., p. 37.

64. S. Banerjee, *Principles and Practice of Management*, New Delhi, Oxford and IBH Publishing Co, 1982, p. 38.

65. R. Pettinger, *Introduction to Management*, op. cit., p. 15.

66. R. Pettinger, *Introduction to Management*, op. cit. p. 16.

67. Cf. L.J. Peter, *The Peter Principle*, London, Penguin, 1970.

68. R. Pettinger, *Introduction to Management*, op. cit. p. 17

69. The following are his important writings: 1) The Human Side of Enterprise, New Delhi, TMH, 1977; 2) The Professional Manager; 3) Leadership and Motivation

70. Cf. V.P. Michael, *Perspective Management*, op. cit., pp. 68-70.

71. Urwick's ideas are expressed mainly in his work, Namely *Elements of Administration*, London, Pitman, 1947.

72. D.R. Hampton, *Management*, op. cit., p. 56.

73. D.R. Hampton, *Management*, op. cit., p. 58.

74. Chester I. Bernard, *The Functions of the Executive*, Cambridge, Mass: Harvard University Press, 1938.

75. Chester I. Bernard, *The Functions of the Executive*, Cambridge, Mass: Harvard University. Press, 1938, p. 8 as Quoted by R.N. Singh, Management Thought and Thinkers, Sultan Chand and Sons, New Delhi, p. 177.

76. Rensis Likert, *New Patterns of Management*, New York, McGraw-Hill Book Company, 1961.

77. Cf. H. Koontz and H. Weihrich, *Management*, op. cit., p. 443.

78. Cf. H. Koontz and H. Weihrich, *Management*, op. cit., p. 417.

79. Cf. George C. Homans, *The Human Group*, New York, Harcourt, Brace and Company, 1950, p. 79ff
80. D.R. Hampton, Management., op. cit., pp. 369-370.
81. The findings of these authors have appeared in the book co-authored by them: *The Social Psychology of Organisations*, New York, John Wiley and Sons, 1966.
82. S. Banerjee, Principles and Practice of Management, op. cit., p. 462.
83. Ibid.
84. G. Burton and M. Thakur, *Management Today: Principles and Practice*, op. cit., p. 546.
85. G. Moorhead and R. Griffin, *Organisational Behaviour*, Boston, Houton, Mifflin, 1969.
86. G. Burton and M. Thakur, *Management Today: Principles and Practice*, op. cit, p. 546.
87. H. Koontz and H. Weihrich, *Management*, op. cit., p. 137.
88. H. Koontz and H. Weihrich, *Management*, op. cit, p. 136.
89. J.W. Forrester, *Industrial Dynamics*, New York, The MIT Press and John Wiley and Sons, 1961.
90. S. Beer, *Decision and Control*, New York, John Wiley and Sons, 1966.
91. R.L. Ackoff and E.L. Arnoff, *Introduction to Operations Research*, New York, John Wiley and Sons, 1957
92. Lallan Prasad and S.S. Gulshan, *Management: Principles and Practices*, New Delhi, S. Chand & Company Ltd, 1982, p. 31.
93. G. Burton and M. Thakur, Management Today, Principles and Practice, op. cit, p. 52.
94. Ibid.
95. R.N. Singh, Management Thought and Thinkers, op. cit., p. 113.
96. Ibid.
97. Cf. G.A. Cole, *Management Theory and Practice*, London, DP Publications, 1996, p. 3.
98. Cf. G.Burton and M.Thakur, *Management Today, Principles and Practice*, op.cit.,1996, p. 56.

2

Different Approaches to Management

In the previous chapter we were attempting to show the ways through which management travelled to reach the status of an art and a science. But all those who gave serious thinking on management have not approached this science and art in the same way. The history of management thought includes different emphases and stresses, some of which are one sided and consequently harmful. In this chapter of the thesis we are attempting an overview of the different approaches and an evaluation of the same. All these approaches have their positive qualities and are therefore recommendable. At the same time all the positive qualities alone do not make any approach perfect and flawless. Management is a science that deals not with the things only but mainly and specifically with people. Moreover, it is the fact that it deals with human beings that makes the discipline of management science and art a complex and complicated one. Some of the approaches to management can be listed as follows. We undertake also an evaluation of these approaches so that the more expedient and the more suited can be accepted.

Case Approach

This may also be called the empirical approach. This approach is based on the principle "learn by doing". Here the manager is not trained for his job. Rather he learns by doing things. The manager gets involved in the different activities of the firm or company or institution; he plans, he sees his plan executed; he guides the people, controls them and instructs. In the course of all these he may commit mistakes, but he corrects them in the next chance; then he applies certain other techniques and evaluates the merits of the second over the first and fixes whatever he sees to be the most successful. This is called the case approach because it is from each case the viability and the workability of the approach is found out.

This approach has its merits especially because the manager learns from his own experiments. Another merit of this approach is the possibility of drawing certain common principles out of the past experience, which can be a guide to the manager in the future. At the same time this approach cannot be presented as a scientific approach to other people. Something that happened in the life of one particular manager need not happen in the same way in the life of another manager. People are different. Their behaviour also differs depending on those with whom they work. As H. Koontz and H. Weihrich correctly commend, "this approach has serious limitations in developing management theory and techniques simply because experience has definite limitations" and therefore it cannot scientifically be used "in a subject as complex and broad as management"[1] This means, with this approach we cannot derive certain or sure knowledge of how a group of people behaves with the person placed above them.

This approach has another problem. From what we have learnt from one group of people we cannot predict the behaviour of another group. There is no guarantee that all groups of people will behave in the same way in similar circumstances. The behaviour of people depends very much on education, ideology, faith, value system and personal training.

Inter-personal Behaviour Approach

This approach takes as its starting point the presupposition that management is basically getting things done through people. To make people do as expected and demanded by the manager, it is the interpersonal relationship that is the most important. The manager has to understand the people and the people have to understand the manager. There is need for inter-personal relationship among the employees and between the employees and the manager. Therefore what is needed is a psychological training for all sorts of people involved. Various experiments have been done to give psychological training to the manager and produce the maximum effect. As G.R. Terry and S.G. Franklin put it,

> ... the experiments discovered that if supervisors developed effective human relations skills in counselling employees and established their authority on the basis of social skills and securing co-operation among employees, rather than just technical and coercive expertise, employee productivity was greatly enhanced.[2]

This approach is based on the principle that behavioural sciences like psychology – very specially group psychology and social psychology – and sociology when applied in management will increase productivity. Different contributions have come out from this approach. For example, it teaches how to handle a conflict arising from certain situations in a firm or a company. There can be a situation where the employees are divided on the basis of language, religion or some other dividing factor. This division can grow into great magnitude affecting the productivity of the institute. If the manager is properly trained in human behaviour he can very easily handle the situation and solve the problem of conflict.

There is another positive factor in this approach. This approach takes into consideration the influence the environment can have on the behaviour of people. If a minimum of facilities is not provided in the work place we cannot expect sincere co-operation from the part of the employees and successful running of the firm. Therefore if the manager is properly trained he will see to this problem and try to solve it, with the effect that productivity is increased.[3]

Another area this approach has highlighted is the views of authority. If the manager is too much authoritative and forgets principles of peaceful and healthy human interaction, whatever be his expertise he will only be a failure. Group psychology will tell him how to behave gently, humanly and affectionately to the effect that he instils new spirit and enthusiasm in the workers.[4] In this regard the finding of V.H. Vroom is an eye opener. "The key point of his theory is that an individual's behaviour is formed not on objective reality but on his or her, subjective perception of that reality. The core of the theory...relates to how a person perceives the relationship with the three things—effort, performance and rewards."[5]

In spite of these positive qualities of this approach it has its imperfections. This is not to say that psychology is not useful for effective management nor can we say that the manager need not be a good leader. As H.Koontz and H. Weihrich correctly observe

> ... no one can deny that managing involve human behaviour or dispute that the study of human interactions whether in the context of managing or elsewhere is useful and important. It would likewise be a mistake not to regard leadership and ability to motivate others as important for effective managing.[6]

At the same time this approach does not give due importance to the planning and other factors involved in the effective managing of an institution. This approach with its over emphasis on behavioural sciences unconsciously equates management with psychology. Accordingly it will amount to saying that the best psychologist is the best manager. But our experience from actual life shows that it is far from the truth.

Group Behaviour Approach

The group behaviour approach, though it seems to be closely related to interpersonal behaviour approach, is not the same. In fact, this approach is the result of concerted efforts made by many social and behavioural scientists to eliminate the inadequacies and drawbacks associated with the interpersonal behaviour approach. It gives due importance to the behaviour of people in groups rather than behaviour of individuals as individuals or in their relationship with other individuals. When we use the term group behaviour, we refer to the disciplines of sociology, social psychology and anthropology. Sociology attempts to isolate, define and describe human behaviour in groups. It opens the door to develop laws and generalisations about human nature, social interaction, customs, and social organisation. One of the main contributions of sociologists in relation to management is the recognition of informal groups and their importance in an organisation. They also provide insights to managers regarding leader and follower roles and how patterns of power and authority are applied in organisations. Social psychology is another important discipline, which play an important role in the group behaviour approach. Social psychology deals with behaviour as it relates to other individuals. It studies how groups and individuals influence and modify one another's behaviour. Human behaviour is very complex and as soon as a person gets into a group, he/she starts behaving differently. The reason is that the pattern of behaviour is guided and governed by group dynamics. Anthropology examines the behaviours of people, including the social, technical, and family behaviours that are part of the broad concept of culture. The study of cultural anthropology, which analyses the different peoples, and cultures of the world is also very important in the human behaviour approach, because the ways in which the individuals behave, the priority of needs they attempt to satisfy, and the means they choose by which to satisfy them are all functions of culture. In the present industrial world, where the number of females and foreign-born workers are increasing, cultural anthropologists inform managers that different people from different backgrounds and cultures will have to be integrated into the organisations.[7]

We can see a number of positive values in the group behaviour approach. Sociology and social psychology have had great impact in shaping management thought. Cultural anthropology has made significant contributions regarding the effect of culture on organisations. As compared to interpersonal behaviour approach, the group behaviour approach seems to be broader because it is properly concerned about technological aspect of job, group dynamics, leadership, communication, motivation etc. The fact that a group has an identity of its own over and above the sum total of the members who constitute the group is a valuable insight and is being recognised by all social scientists. Therefore, it is absolutely necessary that the manager be conscious of the group behaviour and not be aware of the behaviour of individuals as individuals. At the same time those who apply this valid insight in the science of management seems to forget that management is much more than mere group behaviour.

Co-operative Social Systems Approach

This approach has as its root the presupposition that the organisations are to be understood as systems. But what is a system? In general "a system is some organised whole…made up of parts connected in some fashion...and directed to some purpose."[8] But organizations are not simple systems. Often they are "complex social systems responsive to a number of interdependent and important variables."[9] The important variables that decide a system are people, technology, organisation structures and environment. The studies of many researchers have contributed to this approach to management. For example we have the findings of Chester Bernard. His book, *The Functions of Executive* is very famous in this regard. According to him management has to do with social systems.

The system understanding is very helpful for the managing of organisations because it "simplifies to some degree, understanding the multitudinous activities with which a manager must work and it also enables the management to see better the nature of the complex problems to be solved."[10] But what is a social system? According to Bernard, social system is "the co-operative interaction of the ideas, forces, desires and thinking of two or more people."[11] This social system is an organisation and organisation is defined as "systems of interdependent activity encompassing at least several primary groups and usually characterised at the level of consciousness of participants by a high degree of rational direction of behaviour towards ends that are objects of common knowledge."[12]

The view that management has to do with social systems where different strata of individuals have to work together in a co-operative spirit is a valid view and it helps to highlight the importance of the organisational character involved in it. All managers do in fact "operate in a co-operative social system". But the problem with this approach is that it unduly generalises certain things. Everything that works together need not always be an organisation. The same way all that has to do with co-operation need not be managed. A family may be celebrating the matrimonial anniversary of the parents. Different individuals have different roles to play here. But does this get together necessarily need a formal management? Or the thousands of vehicles running through the street are working together in a sense. But are we to call it an organisation? Therefore it seems that, in spite of the new insights, which the co-operative social systems approach provides, it is not a perfect and a flawless approach. There is over simplification and undue generalisation in this approach.

Composite Longwall Method Approach

This is another approach to management. Though there are many researchers who approach management from a social technical systems perspective, this approach is generally attached to E.L. Trist and those who worked with him. Specially to be mentioned is the article, which appeared in "*Human Relations*", co-authored by himself and K. Bamforth. The article was entitled 'Some Social and Psychological Consequences of the Longwall method Coal Getting'.[13] The important contribution of this approach is that it brings to light an often-neglected aspect of social system. In the previous approaches especially Co-operative Social System and Inter-Personal Relationship approach an organisation was seen mainly from the personal and behavioural perspectives. In those approaches the technical system, that is, the system constituted by non-human factors was not properly taken care of. But E.L.Trist and his companions argued with evidences that a technical system can fundamentally influence the behaviour of persons and their effectiveness. On the basis of this finding they argued that in an organisation we have to take into consideration two levels of system, one is the system constituted by persons and the other is the system constituted by non-human factors.

To explain the findings of Trist and his associates, it is good to have a bird's eye view of the stages through which coal mining passed in the 1940s and afterwards. Before the contribution of Trist and others came, coal had been extracted by isolated groups of individuals. They worked at a very slow pace and the effectiveness depended only on the peaceful atmosphere that existed in the mines. But there were frequent outbursts of anger and it affected the productivity. Then came coal-cutters and mechanical conveyors. This new situation totally affected the productivity as well as the atmosphere within the mines. And the result was disastrous. As Cole puts it—

> ...the social consequences of the new method arising from the breakdown of the previously closely-integrated social structure were: increased haggling overpay, inter-shift competition for the best jobs, the seeking of scapegoats in other ships and a noticeable increase in absenteeism.[14]

The conclusion is inevitable that technical system alone cannot guarantee effectiveness. Rather it should go hand-in hand with other systems. It is in the light of Trist and Associates that the composite Longwall method was introduced, where there is a healthy mingling of social system and technical system.

This system has all the positive aspects of Co-operative social system as well as the conveniences resulting from technical system. At the same time we cannot close our eye towards the negative side of this approach. Here everything is seen solely from the point of view of systems and no thought is given to skills, strategies, staffing and so on. In fact the effectiveness of a system depends on these factors also.

Decision Theory Approach

This is another approach to management. Here the emphasis is on decision-making. This approach can be explained in the following way. In every management the person in charge has to take a number of decisions everyday. Decision-making itself can be defined as selecting one from many possibilities. The person who makes decision chooses one from many possible courses of actions. Depending on the correctness of the decision the whole process of management will prove to be successful or not. Therefore, decision-making is of utmost importance in management. Hence, some thinkers and researchers approach management from the perspective of decision-making. Though the decision is vital, these thinkers do not concentrate on decision alone. Rather they take into consideration those things which are directly or indirectly related to decision-making, especially those that follow decision-making. But they believe that the central focus can be given to decision-making.[15] This approach is something commendable because as Terry and Franklin say—

> Almost all-human activity is now considered legitimate for a decision-making study. To illustrate, decisional adherence have grappled with decisions pertaining to the diagnosis and prescriptions for improving communications, incentives, and the reactions of the individual to a group.[16]

In spite of the positive aspects of this approach it cannot be qualified as an integral approach because it is a too narrow approach to identify management with decision-making. There are other aspects in management like the system, the personnel etc. Though decision can influence all these areas there cannot be a total identification between many of these areas and decision-making itself.

Systems Approach

The systems approach to management is really a way of thinking about management problems. It views an organisation as a group of interrelated and therefore, interdependent parts with a single purpose. The basic idea of systems approach is that because the action of one-part influences the others, managers cannot deal separately with individual parts. It is an integrating approach, which considers management in its totality based on empirical data. The term system may be defined as "an organised or complex whole; an assemblage or combination of things or parts forming a complex unitary whole."[17] These parts may also be viewed as subsystems of a larger system. It is only through these subsystems the larger system operates. Here the larger system can be viewed as a whole entity or totality. The various subsystems involved in the functioning of the larger one are closely related to each other and to the larger system as a whole. These subsystems interact with each other by influencing others and getting influenced by them. Every system has subsystems and every subsystem may be considered as a system because it may have subsystems.[18]

Thus the system approach defines organisation as a complex whole consisting of mutually interdependent and interacting parts, which are described as subsystems. Assuming that whole is greater than the sum of its parts, this approach is considered as holistic in nature.

Systems may broadly be classified into four categories—physical, mechanical, biological and social. Physical systems are inevitable parts of nature. For example solar system, seasons, rivers, etc. The devices, which are innovated or invented by human beings for their betterment, are termed as mechanical systems. These systems based on technology are totally closed systems in nature, as they do not interact with external environment. Such mechanical systems are, for example, machines, motor cars, electric appliances and consumer durables etc. The systems, which regulate and control existence and survival of all living species like humans and plants, are known as biological systems. Social systems can be described as those systems, which have been developed by human beings to facilitate cooperative working and to overcome the problem of isolation and desolation. All types of organisations whether small or big, formal or informal, economic or non-economic belong to social system.[19]

Depending on the interaction with external environment, a system may either be a closed system or an open system. Most of the physical and mechanical systems are closed systems since they do not interact with external environment and they are self-sustained in nature. On the other hand, biological and social systems are relatively open systems as they interact with external environment on regular basis and depend on it for the supply of necessary inputs.

An organisation, since it interacts with external environment and its existence depends on its ability to cope with changing environment is considered relatively as an open system. At the same time it has to preserve its identity, maintain stability and protect autonomy. So it is not a complete open system. In this connection Kreitener has rightly pointed out that just as no person is an island, no organisation or organizational subsystem is an island. An organisation is basically an input-output system since it gets various inputs, both physical and human, such as land, capital, building, raw material, machine, technology, labour and management from the society. The organisation supplies back the output received in the form of goods and services to the society. The feedback in the form of valuable information given by the society helps the organisation to adjust the system in such a way, that it may be more responsive to the needs of the society.

Systems approach possesses the conceptual level of managerial analysis much higher than any other approach. It helps the managers to recognise that organisations are systems made up of interdependent parts and that a change in one part affects the other parts. This awareness will force the manager to view the organisation as a dynamic whole and will try to anticipate the intended and unintended impacts of their decisions. Thus, when managers plan, they have no choice but to consider such external variables as markets, technology, social forces, laws and regulations. Intelligent and practical managers see their problems and activities as a network of interrelated elements with daily interaction between environments inside or outside their companies.[20] In spite of its positive points this approach, in no way, is the unified theory of management. It is purely theoretical, conceptual, vague and abstract. It cannot be applied successfully to practical situation. The system approach does not offer any tool and technique for analysis and synthesis of various subsystems.

Quantitative or Mathematical Approach to Management

In the modern management thinking quantitative approach, which is also known as operations research approach, management science approach or mathematical approach, has an important role to play. According to this approach all the relevant factors are related to the problem of notations and signs. In order to determine the effect of change in the variables, values of each variable can be worked out with the help of incorporating changes. Computers would be of much use in such situations. After many such exercises the management team can adopt a rational decision-making for a particular problem. Now-a-days a number of such techniques are used for decision-making in management. The most significant among them are linear programming, econometric models, game theory, co-efficient correlation and regression models, queuing theory, simulation, probability etc. Managerial problems related to capital budgeting, cash flow management, production scheduling, product development strategies, inventory control, transportation problems etc are solved by the application of quantitative techniques. Operations research has attained greater importance now-a-days as a result of electronic data processing and computer application.

However, in spite of its publicity, we are still in doubt about its practical application for solving the problem in the realm of business in a big way. In fact many decision-makers make use of past experiences, own value judgment, intuitions, traditions, routines, formalities and so on instead of scientific method. Though quantitative approach may be useful in some areas of decision-making, it is inadequate to portray an integrated approach to management since management must deal with both quantitative and qualitative aspects. In fact, qualitative factors are more important on certain matters like corporate image, worker morale, organisational commitment, qualitative performance of the sales people, and so on.[21]

Contingency Approach

Contingency approach is another rational approach incorporating the environmental factors to management thought. The theorists who support this approach attempt to predict the possible relationships between situations, outcomes, variables and actions. Here they stress the interdependence of the various factors involved in the different managerial situations. The concepts received from major schools of management thought are applied to real life situations.

According to this approach it is the manager who has to identify the exact technique to be employed in a particular situation for making the best contribution to the accomplishment of goals. The ability of the manager plays an important role in the success of this particular approach. The more suitable the method, the more result it would produce. There is no specific method suitable for all situations. According to James Stoner, "where workers need to be encouraged to increase productivity, for example, the classical theorist may prescribe a new work simplification. The behavioural scientist may seek to create a psychologically motivating climate and recommend the opposite: work enrichment. But the manager trained in the contingency approach will ask, "Which method will work best here?" If the workers are unskilled and training opportunities and resources are limited, work simplification might be the best solution. With skilled workers, driven by pride in their abilities, a job enrichment programme might be more effective."[22]

This approach has the positive aspect of considering the environment in which it operates, the technique or method to be used in the given situation, the contingency relationship between them etc. Because of the existence of many alternate choices, it gains importance in the changing business environment of today. It is a bare truth that, given certain characteristics of a job and certain characteristics of people doing the job, specific management practices tend to work better than others. For example, rigid plans, clearly defined jobs, autocratic leadership, and tight controls have at times resulted in high productivity and satisfied workers. At other times, the opposite characteristics (general plans, vaguely defined jobs, democratic leadership, and loose controls) have produced the same results. This is the main reason for the popularity of contingency approach over the last two decades.[23] But this approach also has failed to incorporate all the aspects of systems theory. There is not much that is new in the contingency theory. When Fayol put forward 14 principles of management he also had suggested the flexibility of its application. Through a close examination we can understand that his flexibility is the same thing as what is now presented as contingency. Contingency theory can therefore be considered as "old wine in a new bottle."[24]

Managerial Roles Approach

One of the merits of this approach is that it is one of the recent approaches to management study and it has got popularity in many circles of management research. It is Professor Henry Mintzberg who popularised this approach to management study. 'Observe and then come to conclusion'—is the principle used in this approach. Henry Mintzberg studied the activities of five chief executives and came to this conclusion. The chief executives were chosen from widely different organisations. In the classical classification of managerial functions planning, organising, coordinating and controlling are the functions of the manager. But the close examinations of the activities of these five executives showed that in actual fact the managers or executives do not act in this way. They do a variety of other functions, which are not listed in the classical classification. Therefore, he found that a new approach is needed for a scientific evaluation of management functions. Henry Mintzberg identified ten such roles in which the manager functions. He makes a distinction between the classical classification and his new approach. He rules out the classical classification qualifying it as 'folklore' that is not scientifically established while he qualifies his own as the scientific approach to management studies. The ten roles in which the manager functions, are grouped into three major roles namely interpersonal roles, informational roles and decisional roles. The major roles and the minor roles, which come under the major roles, can be listed as follows:

Interpersonal Roles

Within this major role Mintzberg identifies three roles in which the manager functions. They are:

Figurehead Role

This is the representative role of the manager. As the head of the institution it is the manager who represents it. So he is the head of the institution and only he can represent it in its totality.

Leader Role

If we understand the organisation or firm as a system, the one who leads everyone involved in the organisation is the manager. So he has the leader role to play in the organisation. As a leader he guides and directs the other persons involved in the functioning of the organisation.

Liaison Role

The manager is the one who functions as a link between his own organisation and the people in the organisations outside. Therefore, he has a liaison role also.

Informational Roles

It is the function of the manager as a person, who receives information, acts upon it and communicates information. Within this major role Mintzberg identifies three sub roles of the manager.

Recipient Role

The manager receives information about the functioning of an enterprise. This information concerns the total functioning as well as the functioning of each part of the organization. It includes information about the positive aspect as well as the negative aspects.

Disseminator Role

What the manager has received as information about the institution is passed on to the other persons involved in the functioning of the organisation. If this is not done the manager would not be able to correct deficiencies and exploit the positive qualities.

Spokesperson Role

Spokesperson means a person who functions as the official transmitter of information about an organisation. It is depending on the information transmitted by the manager that the outside world knows about it and forms opinions of appreciation or depreciation. Therefore this role is very important to project a good image of his organisation.

Decision Making Role

This is the third major role in which a manager functions. This role concerns mainly the decisions, which the manager has to make. It is the decision taken by the manager, which control the functioning of the organisation. Mintzberg identifies four sub roles within this major role.

The Entrepreneurial Role

It is the decision concerning the controlling of the organization. How to control the organisation and to direct it—it is the manager who makes decisions concerning them.

The Disturbance-handler Role

This function of the manager is needed when problems appear in the organisation. It is possible that the normal functioning may be disturbed due to foreseen or unforeseen reasons. The manager has to make the appropriate decision at the appropriate moment to handle the situation.

The Resource Allocator Role

Any organisation depends on the resources, which are used in it. It is the manager who collects resources, both human and non-human and uses them in the proper place. So he has to make decisions about the resources to be used and the manner in which they are to be used.

Negotiator Role

It is concerning the negotiation the manager has to do. In an organisation there are not only persons but also groups of persons and these groups will have different aims, which may lead to conflicts. It is the duty of the manager to solve such problems through negotiations. So he has a negotiator role.

In all these three major roles altogether there are ten roles in which the manager functions—three in the interpersonal role, three in the informational role and four in the decision-making role. It is from his study of the roles in which the manager functions that Mintzberg names this approach as managerial roles approach.

What about the quality of this approach? Is it a perfect approach? From the very outset this approach has faced severe criticism from different corners. First of all we have to ask is the experiment itself scientific? Mintzberg has studied only five sample executives. Are we entitled to make conclusions from a study of mere five executives? Is not this number too small to support this conclusion?

We have also to ask whether this is a new approach or a new name for an old approach. Fayol has already spoken of planning, organising, staffing and so on. What Mintzberg calls the leader role of the manager is nothing but the functioning of leading which Fayol has already identified. What Mintzberg calls the figurehead role seems to be the same as organising in another name. The same criticism can be levelled against all the other roles, which Mintzberg identifies. Therefore, it seems, there is not anything substantially new in this approach. There is yet another problem with this approach. All these roles are not really roles of the manager as manager. For example fund raising also is a function that comes under resource allocator role. Money is one of the resources. Without raising funds one cannot allocate it. Therefore are we to include fund raising also in the role of the manager?

In short this approach lacks both newness and precision. Many of the things Mintzberg presents as new are already included in Fayol's theory. Some of the roles, which Mintzberg presents as manager role, are not strictly manager's role.

Management Process Approach

The basic principle behind this approach is that management functions like any other operational science. An operational science has a system of knowledge pertaining to that particular science and practical techniques which are made use of in bringing about the desired results. Those who approached management in this way recognise that there is a core of knowledge, a system, which pertains to the field of management. This system of knowledge supplies the basic philosophy of management. Then this knowledge is put into practice for achieving the results.

The basic management science and theory properly belongs to management alone. This is the core knowledge. At the same time it has to draw helpful knowledge from other sciences also because in our modern age no science can function in complete isolation from other sciences. Thus in addition to the central core of knowledge pertaining to management, ideas and insights are drawn from other sciences like psychology, sociology, mathematics, decision theory, systems theory and so on. For example the manager has to know what group behaviour is. Therefore he needs knowledge drawn from sociology or social psychology. Yet management is not the joint functioning of so many such sciences. It has its own central core, which is not shared by other sciences. The knowledge drawn from other sciences are examined and evaluated and adapted to the particular needs of the science of management. It "is not interested in all the important knowledge in these various fields but only that which is deemed most useful and relevant to managing."[25]

Management is a very difficult and complex science because it has to deal with diverse situations and peoples. The complexity asks for co-operation with and theoretical help from other sciences. Physical sciences have their role to play in management. Social sciences also are important. Therefore, there is the need for co-operation among the sciences. But this co-operation is to be given and received not with the risk of ruining the identity of management. This approach is something that is built around the basic principles of Henry Fayol, who is recognised as the father of management science. Because of this association with Fayol management process approach is sometimes called the traditional school or the classical school. Moreover, since this approach concentrates on the actual operation of management, i.e. how without losing and endangering its basic principles which pertain to management alone, it draws knowledge from other science and make use of it for achieving the desired results, this approach is also known as the operational approach.

This approach is also not without its problems and limitations. Though it speaks about the central core of knowledge of management it does not give due consideration to co-ordination as a separate function. In fact co-ordination is the essence of management and a manager is appointed in a firm or organisation with the precise end that he would co-ordinate the different functions of the firm. Thus in spite of its positive quality as an approach which seeks the help of other sciences without losing the identity of management this approach also is not perfect.

Conclusion

The different approaches we have so far discussed have their merits and demerits. Each approach is suitable in one or the other situation depending on the nature and size of the business organisation. At the same time these approaches are somewhat narrow in the sense that they have not taken all the aspects of management in its wider form. Of these, some seem to be overused and others underemployed. The task of running large business organisations is not simple. So it is high time that we have to get all the use we can have out of all the methods available. In the modern world management is not limited to doing right things. The suitability of an approach is based on environment, culture and value systems. Often an integral approach with scope for accommodating contextual parameters is found useful. It also includes convincing others that the things being done by the enterprise are right. This demands some extra effort from the part of the organisation and management. So an approach, which accepts a broader and wider vision of management principles and practice, is still to be evolved. The 7-S approach modelled by McKenzie and company after a long period of experimentations seems to be much better than all the previous approaches we have dealt with. We shall discuss this approach in detail in the next chapter.

REFERENCES

1. H. Koontz and H. Weihrich, *Management*, op. cit, p. 40.
2. G.R. Terry and S.G. Franklin, *Principles of Management*, (Eighth Edition), Delhi, Veerendra Kumar Arya, 1991, p. 23.
3. Cf. G.R. Terry and S.G Franklin, *Principles of Management*, op. cit., p. 24.
4. Cf. G. Burton and M. Thakur, *Management Today, Principles and Practice*, Delhi, Tata McGraw-Hill Publishing Company Ltd., 1996 pp. 46-51.
5. G.A. Cole, *Management Theory and Practice*, London, D.P. Publication, 1996, p. 40.
6. H. Koontz and H. Weihrich, *Management*, New York, McGraw-Hill Company, 1988, p. 40.
7. Cf. J.H. Donnelly, J.L. Gibson and J.M. Ivancevich, *Fundamentals of Management*, (Tenth Edition), Boston, Irwin McGraw-Hill, 1998, p. 13.
8. G.R. Terry and S.G. Franklin, *Principles of Management*, op. cit., p. 75.
9. G.A. Cole, *Management Theory and Practice*, op.cit., p. 76.
10. Ibid.
11. H. Koontz and H. Weihrich, *Management*, op. cit., p. 42
12. "Comments on the Theory of Organisations", *American Political Science Review*, Vol. 46, No. 4 (1952), p. 1130.
13. E.L Trist and K. Bamforth "Some Social and Psychological Method of the Longwall method Coal-Getting", *Human Relations*, Vol. 4, No. 1 (1951).
14. G.A. Cole, *Management Theory and Practice,* op. cit, p. 75.

15. H. Koontz and H. Weihrich, *Management*, op. cit., p. 44.

16. G.R. Terry and S.G. Franklin, *Principles of Management*, op. cit., p. 30.

17. L.M. Prasad, *Principles and Practice of Management*, Sultan Chand and Sons, New Delhi, 2001, p. 68.

18. Cf. B.S. Moshal, *Organisation and Management*, New Delhi, Galgotia Publishing Company, 1998

19. Ibid.

20. H. Koontz and H. Weihrich, *Management*, op. cit., p. 44.

21. Cf. V.P. Michael, *Perspective Management*, Bombay, Himalaya Publishing House, 1994, p. 89

22. James A.F. Stoner, *Management*, New Delhi, Prentice Hall of India, 1985, p. 54.

23. Cf. J.H. Donnelly J.L. Gibson and J.M. Ivancevich, *Fundamentals of Management*, op. cit., p. 19.

24. Ibid.

25. H. Koontz and H. Weihrich, *Management*, op. cit., p. 50.

3

The Seven-S Approach

In the previous chapter we were attempting to make an overview of the different management approaches and to evaluate the same. From the evaluation it becomes clear that each of these approaches overemphasise one aspect or other to bring out the problems of management and tries to give solution for the same. In their effort to give solution for one particular problem they discard some other important aspects of management which also should be given due consideration. In the ultimate analysis it is clear that none of these approaches that we have already dealt with gives a perfect and complete solution for the varied problems of management. Our observation is shared by many researchers. For example, the two surveys, conducted at UK by name *The Making of Managers* otherwise known as *Handy Report* and *The Making of British Managers* published in 1987 shed light with regard to educating and training managers in the developed countries. The Handy Report showed that, "There is no single universal way of educating and training managers in the developed countries of the world. It concluded that it was important for a country to check the system best suited to its culture."[1] The two surveys taken together also point to the same direction. Tim Hannagan says, "The two surveys, *The Making of British*

Managers and *The Making of Managers*, suggest that UK has not developed any widely used, clearly understood method for educating and training its managers. In fact, this training was found to be considered as an individual affair to some extent. Individuals certainly regarded their managerial career as their own property, rather than that of their employers."[2]

Management is concerned about places, things and persons. The problems in relation to place and things are more or less predictable and so the manager can handle them easily. But man is a complex being and handling man is not an easy job. Then there is the problem of sophistication resulting from the complexity of organisations in the modern world. The problems facing organisations in the modern world are quite different from those of the bygone years. The specific problems are "competing globally, embracing change, competing through e-commerce, managing knowledge and information, supporting diversity, and maintaining high standards of ethics and social responsibility."[3] It is in this context that many management thinkers attempted to develop some modern approaches to deal with the problem. Among these modern approaches the one developed by the McKenzie Company in the name of 7-S approach or the 'concept of excellence' seems to be better than all other approaches.

Researches Leading to 7-S Approach

The problem of one sidedness and undue overemphasis on any one particular aspect which were characteristics of management thinking in the fifties, sixties and seventies are well recognised by a good number of management thinkers. They were not satisfied with the management practices, which prevailed in Western countries, especially in America, where the best management practices are supposed to be followed. The academic journals, the business press, and the popular media also supported this view and their common impression about the American enterprises was— "Top managements, the business schools that train them, and the consultants who advise them have all been faulted for a destructive preoccupation with analytical technique—too narrow in its conception and too short term in its application."[4] Richard Pascale and Anthony Athos took this criticism seriously and attempted to study the truth behind the criticism. In their attempt they tried to find what has gone wrong with American management and how the management thinking can be refreshed. In their long years of research they could experience the superb quality of Japanese management. They found the statement made by Takeo Fujisawa, co-founder of Honda Motor Company to be correct to a large extent. When asked to compare Japanese and American management he said: "Japanese and American management is 95 per cent the same and differs in all important respects."[5] Pascale and Athos concentrated on this 5 per cent difference in Japanese and American management. Keeping this statement in mind they made a comparative study of a number of companies both in Japan and Western countries. Their study was so extensive that they covered many other international corporations also. Their research led to the creation of a best-selling book by name *'The Art of Japanese Management'* wherein they articulated the key components of success in enterprise. They presented these key components with the title 'Seven-S'. We shall see these components in detail later. The authors made a comprehensive research in collaboration with the international consultants McKenzie's where Tom Peters and Robert Waterman also were members. These two also joined hands with the research made by Pascale and Athos on the characteristics of excellent companies. They drew lessons mainly from America's best-run companies. Their enquiry made them to write another best selling book by name *'In Search of Excellence'*.

The Concept of Excellence

The concept of excellence, which is the product of research made by Tom Peters and Robert Waterman, members of the International Consulting Company McKenzie was a reaction to the experience that the conventional methods and approaches were not bringing the expected result. About this concept Richard Pettinger says:

> "The genesis of the work that subsequently grew into the management concept of 'excellence' was a review carried

out in the later part of the 1970s by McKenzie, the International Management Consulting Firm, of it's thinking and approach to business strategy and organisation effectiveness. This review was itself founded in dissatisfaction with conventional approaches to these matters."[6]

The study was conducted in 62 organisations selected from all sectors of US Industry and Commerce and from many other firms outside the US. Tom Peters and Robert H. Waterman have recorded their experience and new findings in the book titled '*In Search of Excellence*'. In their words,

> "The project showed, more clearly than could have been hoped for, that the excellent companies were, above all, brilliant on the basics. Tools didn't substitute for thinking. Intellect didn't overpower wisdom. Analysis didn't impede action. Rather, these companies worked hard to keep things simple in a complex world. They persisted. They insisted on top quality. They fawned on their customers. They listened to their employees and treated them like adults. They allowed their innovative product and service "champions" long tethers. They allowed some chaos in return for quick action and regular experimentation."[7]

As part of their search for excellence, they made a survey of the companies, which could be qualified as excellent. But then there was the problem of defining excellence itself. i.e., they asked themselves what are the characteristics, which mark out a company as excellent. From their observations of the best performing companies, they identified eight characteristics or attributes of excellent companies. The attributes are:

1. A bias for action
2. Close to the customer
3. Autonomy and entrepreneurship
4. Productivity through people
5. Hands-on, value driven

6. Stick to the knitting
7. Simple form, lean staff
8. Simultaneous loose-tight properties

1. A bias for action

Organisations that follow this principle always undertake action-oriented programmes. They give more stress to actions than to a number of procedures. They believe that "the key success factor in business is simply getting one's arms around almost any practical problem and knocking it off-now."[8]

2. Close to the customer

These companies are so close to the customers that they "get their best product ideas from the customers"[9] themselves.

3. Autonomy and Entrepreneurship

Accordingly, a company, which comes under excellence, allows its members to use their imagination in all possible directions. It never places any restriction on their creativity. It always encourages practical risk taking and supports their good endeavours.

4. Productivity through people

The excellent companies do not regard capital investment as the fundamental source of efficiency improvement. Rather they take each individual as an asset, respect him or her and believe in their contribution to the organisation.

5. Hands-on, value driven

This point clearly explains the basic philosophy that the manager should be an effective leader who has "ideas at the highest level of abstraction and actions at the most mundane level of detail."[10] Accordingly a manager has to instil values through his deeds rather than words. Immediate attention needs to be given both to ideas and its implementation.

6. Stick to the knitting

It explains that an organisation should know the business for which they are best suited and most successful and stick on to such business. In other words an enterprise can make improvement only if it continues, without leaving its main function traditionally adhered to.

7. Simple form, lean staff

These companies prefer simple structural forms for organisation with lean top-level staff.

8. Simultaneous loose-tight properties

Organisations that follow this principle allow the "co-existence of firm, central direction and maximum individual autonomy."[11] Here though the enterprise gives maximum freedom to their members, it will also have rigid control over them.

These eight attributes emanated from the research conducted by Peters and Waterman became the fundamental criteria for benchmarking a company as excellent or otherwise. In this way the two researches made by the consultants of McKenzie Company paved the way to the formulation of a new approach in management known by the name McKenzie's 7-S Approach.

The Different Items in the 7-S Approach

The 7-S framework is gaining popularity in recent years. It is a useful framework for analysing the strategic attributes of an organisation. The art and science of management is fundamentally structured to rest on seven pillars, which constitute its support and strength. These pillars are denoted as Seven Ss. The Seven Ss are strategy, structure, systems, style, staff, shared values and skills. One of the most outstanding features of the 7-S model is that it has been tested extensively by McKenzie Consultants in their studies of many companies. At the same time, well known business schools, such as Harvard and Stanford, have used this framework. Thus theory and practice seem to support each other in the study of management.[12] Each of the 7Ss can be elaborated as follows:

Strategy

Strategy stands as the first item in the 7-S framework suggested by McKenzie. The word strategy is derived from the Greek word strategos, which means "a general". Originally this has been widely used as a military term to mean the art and science of directing military forces. Today, the term is very common in business "to describe the steps taken by an organisation in achieving its objectives and mission."[13] Most organisations have a number of options before them and strategy is concerned with deciding which option is to be used in a particular situation. In other words "strategy is the determination and evaluation of alternatives available to an organisation in achieving its objectives and mission and the selection of the alternative to be pursued."[14]

By means of strategy an organisation gives a clear picture of what kind of enterprise is envisioned and explains how it will attain its vision and respond to the threats and opportunities of the new media. In other words strategies furnish a framework for guiding thought and action. It concerns the direction in which human and material resources will be applied in order to increase the chance of achieving selected objectives.

Some authors divide strategy into business unit strategy and corporate strategy. The first of these may be defined as "the process of developing strategy for a single, largely self-contained business."[15] For a proper understanding of this strategy we have to know what a business unit means. It may be defined as "a whole firm in a small or medium-sized company, or a separate, largely autonomous part of a larger firm, comprising a profit centre that has its own set of external customers and competitors."[16] Now a business strategy is defined as, "How a firm intends to compete in a particular business is called a business strategy. For a single business corporation, corporate strategy is essentially equivalent to business strategy. For a multi business firm, a distinction must be made between the two. ...For business strategy, the conceptual tools generally focus on the structure of an industry and on the dynamics of doing business in that industry."[17]

Corporate strategy is the strategy to be used for the centre, which holds together many business units. But this has to be properly understood. Very often the centre, which holds together different business units, does more harm than good. Those factors, which affects negatively may be listed as follows:

Sometimes the centre makes mistakes and affects the whole firm. The commonly committed mistakes are wrong acquisition, appointing the wrong chief executive or imposing inappropriate controls. Over and above all these the very existence of the centre weakens the responsibility of the business units and those responsible for the running of the business. Therefore, those at the top of the business "behave like managers, not like owners; like bureaucrats, not like entrepreneurs."[18] The history of some of the famous companies reveals that after the abrogation of the centre, the business units could make great advances in sales, income and in every other thing.[19] At the same time this corporate centre has its positive aspects also. In that regard we can speak of six corporate strategies namely[20]—

1. Emergency Corporate Strategy;
2. Olympian Corporate Strategy;
3. Acquisition-Driven Corporate Strategy;
4. Market-Expansion Corporate Strategy;
5 Competency-Based Corporate Strategy; and
6. Performance-Control Corporate Strategy.

By Emergency Corporate Strategy, we mean the role of the centre to intervene in times of disorder in the units and to sort out the causes of the crisis. Olympian Corporate Strategy derives its name from Mount Olympus where the Greek gods resided. These gods never interfere with the affairs of the human beings except when some real need arises. The same way the Chief Executive, the one at the centre, should have other things to do than control the units. He may intervene only at times of crisis. The companies, which follow Acquisition-Driven Corporate Strategy, make frequent and large acquisitions. Such companies should possess both quantitative and qualitative skills like intuition, flair, daring, parsimony, negotiating skills, a good sense of timing, judgement about businesses and those who run them, lateral thinking and also plain commonsense.[21] The Market Expansion Corporate strategy aims at expansion of market in existing markets, the adjacent segments and also to the international level. A truly global outreach is their main objective.

The firm or company, which consider competency as its main objective, may not always be a successful firm or company. But what differentiate them from other firms or companies is the culture, the accumulated learning within parts of the firm, and the quality of the people and the strength of their motivation.[22] Firms or companies, which give due importance to the development of these qualities can be said that they follow competency based corporate strategy. The companies which concentrate on the improvement of the financial performance of the operating companies usually follow performance control corporate strategy.

"Corporate strategy is the pattern of decisions in a company that determines and reveals its objectives, purposes, or goals; produces the principal policies and plans for achieving those goals, and defines the range of business the company is to pursue, the kind of economic and human organisation it is or intends to be, and the nature of the economic and non-economic contribution it intends to make to its share holders, employees, customers and communities."[23]

In deciding on an organisation's future direction, management must answer certain basic questions. Christopher Jerjian explains six steps of planning, which he calls, *The 6 What's of Strategic Planning*. The six steps are the following:

What business are you in?

This relates to the development of a clear vision and mission. Vision means, "A statement of what your organisation will look like". Mission means, "How the vision will be achieved during a specific time-frame".

Wnat is your modus operandi?

This "covers the areas of values, climate and culture. Values can be measured in terms of how you treat your customers, your employees, your suppliers, your shareholders, your community and your competitors. Climate and culture can be seen in terms of how you handle conflict and change".

What is your current position?

It means identifying one's strength, weaknesses, opportunities and threats.

What do you want to become?

It means "a base strategy with focus".

What must you make happen?

It refers to the implementation of the plans.

What criteria can you use to measure your performance?

By establishing benchmarks one can measure performance. Quarterly reports are needed for this.[24]

A failure in strategic planning will seriously affect the successful functioning of a business firm and it will even endanger the very existence of the firm.

In an article by name "*HR key to DTI's Vision*", Zoe Roberts and Karen Higginbottom report about the loss incurred by the UK economy calculated at £ 88 billion. It is a typical example of inefficient strategic planning and the study showed that "UK companies waste 85 out of 225 working days per employee through mismanagement and other inefficiencies."[25] It is also found that "the factors that prevent people from working at their most efficient rate include low morale, inappropriate qualifications, IT problems and poor communication."[26]

The strategy formulation affects almost all aspects of a business establishment. The recent survey conducted by CIPD reveals that there is a high rate of labour turnover in industries, which affects organizational performance negatively. Charles Cotton, CIPD adviser, in an article by name,

"A Bit of Positive Spin", suggests a number of steps to solve this problem. "However, the CIPD advises that employers take a more strategic approach to recruitment and retention. They should start spinning a web that attracts, retains, and motivates staff."[27]

Commenting on Kenichi Ohmae's Book *'The Mind of Strategist'*, Trevor Merriden says, "if creativity and intuition are the key, then the central thrust of Ohmae's argument is that successful strategies result not from rigorous analysis but from a particular state of mind. 'In strategic thinking', he argues, 'one first seeks a clear understanding of the particular character of each element of a situation and then makes the fullest use of human brain power to restructure the elements in the most advantageous way'. Brainpower on its own is not enough. Hence, at the heart of a Japanese management, there is often a single, talented, forceful strategist, who has 'an idiosyncratic mode of thinking in which company, customers and competition merge'. These three C's as Ohmae called them, are all important but, for the Japanese, it is the customer who has always been at the heart of the Japanese approach to strategy. Concern for the customer's needs is commonplace in the west today but back in 1982 it was less evident".

Ohmae gives four steps to success. First is a clear focus on the key factors on the success. The second is to build on superiority by employing technology not currently being exploited by the rivals. The third is to pursue aggressive initiatives that upset 'the rules of the game'. Fourth is to make full use of what Ohmae calls 'strategic degrees of freedom', focusing on areas in which competitors are not involved.[28]

Structure

Structure constitutes the second important item in the 7-S model. We can define structures as "how an organisation breaks down its activities into distinct elements and how these elements are co-ordinated". The structure of an organisation involves arrangement of activities and assignment of personnel to these activities in order to achieve the organisational goals in an efficient manner. Following are the different steps usually taken to build the structure of the organisation.

(i) Determination, identification and enumeration of activities;

(ii) Grouping of similar activities and assigning of activities to different personnel;

(iii) Delegating the authority to perform the assigned functions to the respective persons.

The structure of a business organisation is very often situational *i.e.*, depending on the particular situation of a company or a firm. Therefore, it is not possible to speak of one particular structure as the universally best. Many factors are to be taken into consideration before deciding on the particular structure or departmentising to be used in an organisation. "There is no one best way of departmentizing applicable to all organisations and all situations. Managers must determine what is best by looking at the situation they face, the jobs to be done and the way they should be done, the people involved and their personalities, the technology employed in the department, the users being served, and other internal and external environmental factors in the situation."[29]

This situational approach to structure comes from the very nature of it. Structure is not an end in itself, but a means for achieving an end. As means the best one is that which is most capable of achieving the end. Since there is no universally best structure we can speak of mixing types of departmentation. That means some of the activities of a company can be put together under one manager and certain other activities under another manager. The structure within each of these will be essentially different and will have freedom to function independently of other groupings. What we do here is that we mix different types of departmentation. But the fact is that many people are unable to see the logic of this type of departmentation. Yet this is a very practical approach. The purpose of this mixing up is "to group activities in the manner which will best contribute to achieving enterprise objectives". Also managers should keep in mind that "if a variety of bases does this, there is no reason why managers should not take advantage of the alternatives before them."[30] On the other hand from an external point of view it may look nice that all the different activities of an organisation or company have identical structure. But from a practical point of view this is not proved to be a success, but a failure.

System

In the 7-S model, system stands as the third important item. A system may be defined as "a group of interrelated parts that function as a whole to achieve a common purpose."[31] Or it can be defined as "a collection of interrelated parts and components that form a whole."[32] Another possible definition is that a system is "a goal oriented organism that is composed of parts interrelated in such a way that the total system is greater than the sum of its parts."[33] In the view of Gary Dessler, a system may be defined as follows:

"Basically, a system is any entity-a hospital, a city, a bank and so on—that has both interdependent parts and a purpose."[34] All systems have four basic characteristics. The first and foremost characteristic is that they all operate within an environment. As far as an organisation is concerned, these may include clients, competitors, unions and Government. Secondly, all systems contain elements, components, or subsystems, which are in the form of basic building blocks of a system. It may consist of various departments like production, finance, sales, or personnel. Thirdly, systems are also characterised by the interrelatedness of their subsystems. Because of this interrelatedness a manager cannot change one subsystem without affecting the rest. Fourthly, all systems have a central function or purpose and on the basis of this purpose its subsystems are evaluated.

According to another view a system is "a set of interrelated and interdependent parts arranged in a manner that produces a unified whole."[35] According to this definition societies are systems. The same way automobiles, animals, human body are all systems. Systems also have three basic elements, namely, inputs, transformational process and output. All of them function within an environment. When applied to business firms those that come under the inputs are materials used, labour and capital. On a larger perspective, we can say that the inputs include "people, capital and managerial skill as well as technical knowledge and skills."[36] Under transformation process come the finished products or the services *i.e.*, the material, labour and capital function together so as to transform all of them into the finished products. Sales may be considered as the output of the system.

There are two types of systems—open and closed. Open systems are those systems, which interact constantly with their environment for their working. The environment consists of several sectors or subdivisions of the external environment like the industry, raw materials, human resources, financial resources, market, technology, economic conditions, government etc.

For the successful survival of an organisation, it should respond positively with all these environmental sectors and though all these elements are outside the boundary of the organisation, these have the potential to affect all or part of the organisation.

The systems which are self-contained and self-sufficient in itself are termed as closed systems. Such systems do not require other interactions to make them work. Such systems are very few in number and domestic central heating systems are examples for closed systems. Even these systems depend on a constant supply of energy to ensure continuity of operation.

From another perspective systems may also be formal systems, informal systems and networks system. Formal system is devised and developed by the organisation itself with specific purposes. An organisation depends on these groups for its effective operation. Whereas an informal system is devised and developed by individuals and groups on an informal style. A network system is a combination of both the formal and informal groups in an organisation. Networks are normally based on human interaction and information exchange. Their intention "is both to support the operations of the organisation and to ensure the continuity and stability of the position of individuals and groups."[37]

Style

Style the next important factor in the 7-S framework, is the philosophy, values and shared beliefs adopted by managers in their use of power. An executive has to lead different types of subordinates and has to adopt different styles for leading them at the workplace according to the nature of the situation. There are different types of management styles like autocratic or authoritarian style, consultative or participative style, democratic style, bureaucratic style, manipulative style, paternalistic style and expert style. The special characteristics of each of these style is explained below:

Autocratic or Authoritarian Style

- Manager or leader makes all final decisions for the group.
- He makes close supervision on subordinates.
- Individual member's interest and opinions is secondary to those of the organisation.
- Manager always places great demands on staff.
- He encourages no questions from subordinates.
- There exists an environment of coerce and threat.

Consultative or Participative Style

- Manager or leader makes decisions only after consultation with the group.
- There is free communication between the manager and members.
- Manager or leader is supportive and developmental.
- He is easily approachable and decisive.
- He encourages questions and enquiries from members.
- He takes all the responsibility and accountability for results.

Democratic Style

- The group makes decisions by consultation or vote.

- The decision taken by the group is to be observed and supported by all the members.
- All the members can actively participate in the group discussion and is bound to contribute to the discussion.
- There is the possibility of development of unions in the organisation by the members.
- Leadership role is assured by the chair.

Bureaucratic Style

- There are predefined rules and regulations in the organisation.
- Both manager and subordinates are bound by these rules, regulations and procedures.
- Here the management is more or less a routine matter.

Manipulative Style

- Manager or leader has certain abilities to exploit the subordinates.
- He makes use of the employees for the attainment of the organisation's objectives and exploits the aspirations of employees for his gain.

Paternalistic Style

- Here the manager maintains a fatherly attitude towards subordinates.
- Both manager and subordinates work together like a family.
- Healthy cooperation and peaceful atmosphere exist in the organisation.

Expert Style

- Leadership is based on the ability, knowledge and competence of the leader.
- Manager is above all the subordinate.
- He has a specific role to play, different from those of the subordinates.

Chris Mahony, speaks about a different management style by name transformational style. In a study on how the local authorities can improve their performance she reports, "Enlightened Councils have long since moved away from transactional styles. The sheer pace and scale of change in the public sector can't be dealt with in command and control mode". She further says, "Transformational styles recognise this and harness individual talents to the benefit of the organisation. It doesn't mean doing your own thing; it means having confident, competent staff who are clear about the type of council they are in and what is expected of them."[38]

Blake and Mouton have suggested another model known as 'managerial grid' wherein they speak of two dimensions of managerial concern. Accordingly, to be effective and successful a manager should have both 'concern for people' and 'concern for production/output'. They argue that concern for the task and concern for the people should be given equal importance and grown alongside each other rather than one being emphasised at the expense of the other.

Contingency approach otherwise known as situational approach is another type of management style. Here the manager should consider the interaction and interrelation between the organisation and environment. This style urges the manager to recognise and accommodate those elements that cannot be controlled. He should also recognise those elements that can be controlled and influenced in different situations. It requires the manager to change the leadership or management style according to the changing nature of the situation.

Tim Hannagan, tho author of *Management Concepts and Practices* speaks about the nature of leader-member relations for an effective running of an organisation. He says,

> "This is the most important factor in leader effectiveness. The degree to which leaders have the confidence, support and loyalty of subordinates is an essential feature of leader effectiveness. When these relations are strong the leader has a firm base from which to influence the behaviour of

subordinates. When the leader-subordinate relation is weak, the influence of the leaders is only through the impersonal authority provided by their position in the organization."[39]

The management style adopted by an executive speaks a lot about the organisation and it determines its success to a greater extent.

Staff

One of the items in the 7-S approach is concerning the staff. Staff or human resource is the most valuable asset of an organisation, and not the money or physical equipment. Human resources is utilised to the maximum possible extent in order to achieve individual and organisational goals. In fact an organisation's performance and productivity are directly in proportion to the quantity and quality of its staff. Staff means that the company has hired able people, trained them well and assigned them to the right jobs. It covers selection, training, reward and recognition, retention, motivation and assignment to appropriate work. Staffs need the skills and aptitude for developing customer relationships, service and sales.

There are different approaches to staff.

Unitary Approach

According to this approach, an organisation takes all the possible steps to harmonise and integrate the individual aims, objectives, hopes, fears, aspirations and ambitions with those of the organisation.

Plural Approach

Under this approach the organisation recognises the divergent and often conflicting aims, objectives and drives of the staff and tries to fulfil their personal and professional needs and through this the organisation aims at the satisfaction of its needs.

Radical Approach

Radical approach, also known as Marxist approach, believes that the long term productive effort and harmony of the staff in the organisation can be ensured by offering them substantial shareholdings in the company for which they work, or substantial profit-sharing arrangements.

Mutual Approach

According to this approach each employee is ranked on the basis of his or her occupational and organisational effectiveness. This approach will work well only if there is full openness and availability of information, knowledge of activities and understanding of the value of every contribution.

Cooperative Approach

Under this approach the organisation establishes a psychological and behavioural basis of partnership and involvement depending on the value of the contribution that everyone is to make.

Confrontational Approach

This is an adversarial approach to staff and is based on the belief that harmony of objectives is impossible. This idea has led to the creation of systems and processes for containing and managing conflict.

In an article Julie Beardwell and Chris Britton stress the essentials of teamwork among staff in the workplace. They say:

> Effective Communication and information sharing are important because open communications about workplace issues indicate high levels of trust. Information about the organisation and its context is also essential for effective teamwork and employee participation. So it seems reasonable to assume that maintaining effective workplace communication and ensuring that employees receive adequate information should be of considerable importance to HR practitioners.[40]

An organisation, which considers human resource as the most valuable asset, will be alert not to hurt the feelings of subordinates. In an article by name, "What it takes", Jerry Useem has stated this fact very clearly. It is like this: "How much emotion should you show your subordinates? The answer: It's okay to show quite a lot. But it's not okay to show fear."[41]

As P.G. Hegde says, "Firms which ignore employee satisfaction are paving the way to their own peril."[42] Almost the same idea is expressed by Raghavendra Rao.He quotes De Koning who says, "There is often a negative correlation between manager evaluation of employee performance and customer evaluation (of the same employees). ...The reason is that managers evaluate on their perceptions of "good citizenship"-whether an employee turns up every day or is pleasant to deal with. On the other hand, great performers are often difficult people. They have egos and attitudes—great performers need great managers (to evaluate them)."[43]

In evaluating and selecting personnel for different jobs there is an oft-repeated mistake of depending only on the directly visible features of an individual. David Cohen in his book, *The Talent Edge*, questions the correctness of this method. He compares the behavioural tendencies of an individual to the different layers of the onion. On the surface there is the layer, which can easily be pealed. This represents the layer of a person's behaviour, which is easy to observe. Below that in the onion there is the deeper layer, which is not so easy to peal. This represents those layers of a personality, which are full of the "can do" factors. An interviewer should be able to find out this layer also. Beneath these truths lies the third layer, which consists of the "will do" factors. The will do factors "are stable and less subject to change."[44]

Shared Values

The next important item in the 7-S concept of excellence is "shared value". These are the basic values and mission of the organisation. Shared values means that the employees share the same guiding values. Values are things that you would strive for even if they were demonstrably not profitable. They rise above profit targets and growth objectives by relating the goals of the firm to deeper human needs and principles. Values act as an organisation's conscience, providing guidance in times of crisis. Shared values and beliefs linked to the goals of the firm are like keys to developing all the other aspects.

M. Davidson Says,

"Values are the rock on which organisations that survive and succeed over the long haul are built. Without them there is no foundation, and, like the house built on sand, organisations without values will be swept away when the winds and the storms of hard times come. But values alone are not enough. We also need purposes, the lighthouse to guide our way. Together values and purposes solve the problem of the company that went ahead with the disastrous venture by providing two vital, overarching and organization-wide disciplines: shared purposes provide FOCUS by driving strategy, and shared values provide CONTROL by guiding implementation."[45]

Values are the absolute standards by which people order their lives. Each individual may have his/her own personal values. To avoid conflict of values at workplace an organisation should set standards of values, which are required to be followed by its employees. An organisation, to be effective, must be capable of harmonising the individual values with that of the organisational values.

Donald N. Sull explains values as "the shared norms that unite and inspire employees. They are established through both statements and actions. ...Strong values can attract great employees, fuel their passion, and build strong bonds of loyalty."[46] There are different types of values like theoretical values, economic values, aesthetic values, social values, value of integrity, political values, religious values, religious and ethical values, prejudicial values etc. Howard Schultz, a very successful manager, now working as CEO of Starbucks writes about his preferences gathered from his long experience. "More than most managers I rely heavily on my instincts about people. Whether I'm hiring a key executive, selecting an investment banker, or assessing a partner in a joint venture, I look for the same kind of qualities most look for in choosing a spouse: integrity and passion. To me, they're just as important as experience and abilities. I want to work with people who don't leave their values at home but bring them to work, people whose principles match my own."[47]

Skills

The importance of skill in management is rather a more recent finding. In earlier days most managers had no training at all. Or had only some training in general knowledge of what management is. This knowledge they gained through attending seminars and diploma courses. There the stress was on what one knows. But recent management thinkers have stressed the importance of skills. Now there is "a shift from awarding qualifications on the basis of 'what you know' to assessing and certifying 'what you can do.[48]

Skills refer to the abilities that the employees need to carry out the Company's strategy. The organisation needs competent people in order to perform difficult tasks to a high standard. Proper training and development ensure people's know-how to do their jobs and stay up-to-date with the latest techniques.

There is a basic difference between skills and competence, though these two words are used interchangeably in common English use. The same way the skills are different from talents or traits or attributes. Competence is related to prior learning, which is intended for future use. Talents are "the aspects of personality that make an individual unique and valuable.[49] Talents are constants. They don't change and remain through out the individual's life. Yet changes can happen with experience and ageing. On the other hand skill is not strictly coming from formal education-rather "they are individual's personal abilities that are applied to particular tasks."[50]

A manager should possess certain interpersonal skills for the successful performance of his daily tasks. R. Pettinger says,

> Managers will therefore apply their interpersonal skills in the following ways. They will never criticise members of staff either in public or on a personal basis when the problem is related to work. ...If it is necessary to criticise somebody's work performance, then it must be done in a clear and straightforward way with the emphasis upon remedy rather than apportioning blame. Effective criticism is always constructive; the end result must be to reinforce the importance of the individual.[51]

Praising employees is a powerful interpersonal skill. This makes the individual concerned feel one with the organisation, as well as respected and important. As far as possible praising should be conducted in public. Manager should also use his interpersonal skill to instil pride and enthusiasm for the job. Other interpersonal skills, for the successful accomplishment of his daily activities are: "the courage of the manager concerned; job knowledge; self control and self-discipline; a sense of fairness and equity; standards of personal conduct and behaviour that reflect the standards required... and a sense of humour."[52]

In an article by name, *"Mr.Big, Don't Get Too Cozy"*, Geoffrey Colvin has pointed out three important skills, which CEOs need to develop in their career. Accordingly "speed is one of the great theme" on which he has to pay attention. "Your competitors, customers, suppliers, and capital providers have continuous, global real-time information about virtually everything that affects your business, and they act on it quickly". The second point is in relation to accountability. Accountability forces people to be responsible in their own positions. "Accountability makes people uncomfortable because it means that employees get fired if they don't deliver". The third point is in connection with execution of plans. The main reason for the failure of CEOs is their inability to execute the things that they wanted to execute. "A big part of executing a plan is choosing the right people to do the real work of carrying it out."[53]

In an article by name, *"Get with the Programme"*, Jon Watkins speaks about the new training programme connected with the BBC after it had interviewed the employees for improvement and collected their opinion. The employees suggested that the managers and the leaders have to improve. According to the suggestion BBC is conducting training programme for managers and leaders. In this programme they have developed six core BBC values and 53 behaviours. One of the values is "Lead more, Manage better". Another is "One BBC-Great things happen when we work together".

BBC is an organisation "where people who manage large number of staff, don't see their role predominantly as that of a administrator. ...They see their main role as programme makers or something else". As a result the organisation wants "to get the ethos of leadership into the BBC. ...To be able to help people realise that it is valuable and worth spending time on, and ... to create an environment where everyone feels empowered, supported and stretched."[54]

As science advances and technology improves we are faced with new situations, which were unknown and unthinkable in the past. The new situation requires new skills to manage the systems. The old laws become obsolete. What happens in BBC is an example for this.

Conclusion

Experimentation with the 7-S framework for management analysis developed by McKenzie and company shows the great effectiveness of the method. It has got much popularity in the management world especially because it became the basis for the research of two best-selling books with titles, *The Art of Japanese Management* and *In Search of Excellence*. The defect of the approach is minimised by the fact that it includes all the key aspects of the management and has shown interrelatedness of the variables. It has all the advantages of a convergent approach, the different perspectives from various angles converging to a focus and clarifying the details, thus allowing the significant data to emerge. Also it is in correspondence with the complexities of human beings. For example, by using the term 'shared values' they point out the necessity of sharing values among the members in the organisation and stress the importance of personal and organisational values for the very existence of an enterprise. Another positive aspect is that McKenzie consultants in many companies have tested this model. Also the two important business schools like Harvard and Stanford have successfully used this model. Thus this approach has taken both theory and practice and it seems to support each other in the study of management. Another simple positive point is that since all the aspects begin with a 'S' it serves as a memory hook. At the same time it has not oversimplified the management theory.

Though the positive qualities are very significant, in our assessment we discover that this 7-S approach has also certain defects. In the effort to begin all the seven aspects with 'S', there is an unnecessary strain at the risk of clarity. With regard to this approach we are still doubtful whether it has taken into consideration all the possibilities of all the management styles probably adoptable in the future. In the light of new situations in politics, new discoveries in science, changing social systems, new situations in business etc. is it applicable and can we expect that the 7-S will solve all the problems of management? These and many other similar questions have to be scientifically approached and solutions found. This task we will take up as we evaluate the whole approach and suggest ways and means for improvement. In the meantime we will explore the Bible and see how the Seven-S approach is employed in the life of the great leaders of the Bible.

REFERENCES

1. Tim Hannagan, *Management Concepts and Practices*, Delhi, Macmillan India Ltd, 1997, p. 630.
2. Ibid.
3. Richard L. Daft, *Organisation Theory and Design*, (7th edn), USA, South-Western Thomson Learning, 2001, p. 7.
4. Richard Tanner Pascale and Anthony G. Athos, *The Art of Japanese Management*, New York, Penguin Books, 1981, p. xiii.
5. Richard T Pascale and Anthony G. Athos, *The Art of Japanese Management,* op. cit p. viii.
6. R. Pettinger, *Introduction to Management*, op. cit., p. 22.
7. Tom Peters and R.H. Waterman, *In Search of Excellence,* Profile Books, London, 2003, p. 13.
8. Tom Peters and R.H. Waterman, *In Search of Excellence,* op. cit., p. 126.
9. Tom Peters and R.H. Waterman, *In Search of Excellence,* op. cit., p. 14.
10. Tom Peters and R.H. Waterman, *In Search of Excellence,* op. cit., p. 287.
11. Tom Peters and R.H. Waterman, *In Search of Excellence,* op. cit., p. 318.

12. Cf. H. Koontz and H. Weihrich, *Management*, op. cit., p. 47.

13. Lloyd L. Byars, *Strategic Management*, New York, Harper Collins Publishers, 1991, p. 13.

14. Ibid.

15. Richard Koch, The Financial Times Guide to Strategy, How to Create and Deliver a Useful Strategy, London, Pearson Education Ltd, 1995, p. 17.

16. Ibid.

17. F.J. Aguilar, *General Managers in Action,* Oxford, Oxford University Press, 1988, pp. 23-24.

18. Richard Koch, *The Financial Times Guide to Strategy, How to Create and Deliver a Useful Strategy,* op.cit. p. 87.

19. Cf. Richard Koch who gives a Case Study of Premier Brands, which could increase its profits ten times higher after destroying the centre. See Richard Koch, p.87

20. Cf. Richard Koch, The Financial Times Guide to Strategy, How to Create and Deliver a Useful Strategy, op. cit.p. 91.

21. Cf. Richard Koch, *The Financial Times Guide to Strategy, How to Create and Deliver a Useful Strategy,* op. cit. p. 104

22. Cf. Richard Koch, *The Financial Times Guide to Strategy, How to Create and Deliver a Useful Strategy*, op. cit. p. 114.

23. K.R. Andrews, *The Concept of Corporate Strategy*, Homewood, III.: RDIrwin, 1980, p. 18.

24. Cf. Christopher Jerjian, "Practice Makes Perfect", *Sales and Marketing Management,* June 1998, pp. 26-27.

25. Zoe Roberts and Karen Higginbottom, "HR Key to DTI's Vision", *People Management,* October 9, 2003, p. 7.

26. Ibid.

27. Cf. Charles Cotton, "A Bit of Positive Spin", *People Management*, Dec. 18, 2003, p. 23.

28. Cf. Trevor Merriden, *Management Today*, Sept. 1998, p. 103.

29. Harold Koontz and Heinz Weihrich, *Management*, op. cit., p. 199-201.

30. Harold Koontz and Heinz Weihrich, *Management*, op. cit., p. 201.

31. J.S. Chandan, *Management Concepts and Strategies*, op. cit. p. 42.

32. R. Pettinger, *Introduction to Management*, op. cit., p. 121.

33. Gene Burton and Manab Thakur, *Management Today*, op. cit. p. 54.

34. Gary Dessler, *Management Fundamentals*, Virginia, Reston Publishing Company, 1995, p. 14.

35. Stephen B. Robins, *Management Concepts and Practices*, New Jersey, Prentice-Hall, 1984, p. 36.

36. Harold Koontz and H. Weihrich, *Management*, op. cit. p. 12.

37. R. Pettinger, *Introduction to Management*, op. cit. p. 122.

38. Chris Mahony, "On Good Authority", *People Management*, March 6, 2003, pp. 29-30.

39. Tim Hannagan, *Management Concepts and Practices*, Delhi, Macmillan India Ltd., 1997, p. 49.

40. Julie Beardwell and Chris Britton, "Look Who's Talking: The Impact of HR on Workplace Communication", *People Management*, 9th October 2003, p. 66.

41. Jerry Useem, "What It Takes", *Fortune*, November 19, 2001, p. 94.

42. P.G. Hegde, "Faulty HR and Banking Chaos", *Indian Management*, Sept. 2003, p. 48.

43. Raghavendra Rao, "Are you Rewarding Right?", *Indian Management*, Jan. 2004, p. 48.

44. P.V.L. Raju, "A Case for Behaviour Interviewing", *HRM Review*, Vol. 3 (Jan. 2003) No: 1, p. 20.

45. M. Davidson, *The Transformation of Management*, Macmillan Press Ltd, London, 1995, p. 109.

46. Donald N. Sull, "Managing By Commitments", *Harvard Business Review*, June 2003, p. 86.

47. Howard Schultz and Dori Jones Yang, *Pour Your Heart Into It*, Published by Hyperion and Reprinted in *Fortune*, Sept. 29, 1997, p. 141.

48. M. Dale, *Developing Management Skills, Techniques for Improving Learning and Performance*, London, Kogan Page, 2003, p. 27.

49. M. Dale, *Developing Management Skills, Techniques for Improving Learning and Performance,* op. cit., p. 28.

50. Ibid.

51. R. Pettinger, *Introduction to Management*, op. cit., p. 581.

52. Ibid.

53. Geoffrey Colvin, "Mr. Big, Don't Get Too Cozy", *Fortune*, Dec.17, 2001, p. 36.

54. People Management, June 12, 2003, p. 14

4

The Seven–S Approach in the Bible

In the previous chapters we concentrated mainly on three important points. Firstly we have seen a short history of management as an art and science. Secondly, we saw the different approaches employed in management discipline. Thirdly we discussed the Seven-S approach, which is one of the most recent approaches accepted by a good number of management thinkers and scholars. Our present task in this chapter and the next is to see how the Seven-S approach is employed in the Bible. We take one example each from the Old Testament, and New Testament of the Bible. In the Old Testament, the person who gave a definite organisational form to the Jewish people and their religion is Moses. He was the one who freed the Jews who were slaves in Egypt and led them through the wilderness of Sinai towards the land of Canaan, which God had promised to give them. Moses gave leadership to the people during their negotiations with Pharaoh, the king of Egypt, got their freedom from slavery and led them through the wilderness up to the land of Moab, on the other side of the river Jordan. During this travel through the wilderness Moses gave them laws for social life and finalised the religion of the people in fidelity to Yahweh, the God who appointed Moses as the leader and guided the people and their leader in all circumstances of difficulty. Since the people achieved liberation through the leadership of Moses, the Movement started by Moses may be termed a Liberation Movement. In this movement Moses acts as an able manager. We will examine his life and activities to see how the method employs is parallel to the Seven-S approach.

The Seven-S Approach in the Liberation Movement of Moses

The Books from Exodus to Deuteronomy (Exodus, Leviticus, Numbers and Deuteronomy) present Moses as the liberator of the people of Israel who were slaves in Egypt under Pharaoh. God sends him to Egypt to free the people from slavery and to lead them to the land of Canaan which God would free from the present occupants like the Canaanites, the Hittites, the Amorites, the Perizzites, the Hivites and the Jebusites and give to the Israelites. Moses does as God commanded him and leads the people out of Egypt. On the way they pass through the wilderness of Sinai where God meets them and makes a covenant with them raising them to the status of the people of God. The people continue their journey after the covenant and reach up to the place called Moab, near the river of Jordan on the other side of which is the land of Canaan, the Promised Land. To get the people out of the land of Egypt Moses had to handle a rough character like Pharaoh and force him to let the people go by performing many miracles, which were plagues, inflicted on Pharaoh and his people, the Egyptians. At the end of a series of ten such plagues Pharaoh is forced to let the people go. On a night of religious importance, the night of Passover, in which the first-born sons of all the Egyptian families including the family of the king died by a mysterious intervention of God, Pharaoh lets the people of Israel go out of the land. It is reported in the Bible in the following words:

> Then he summoned Moses and Aaron in the night, and said, "Rise up, go away from my people, both you and the Israelites! Go, worship the LORD, as you said. Take your flocks and your herds, as you said, and be gone. And bring a blessing on me too!"[1]

Accordingly Moses led the people out of Egypt. On the way they had both the assistance of God and leadership of Moses. God went in front of them "in a pillar of cloud by day" and "in a pillar of fire by night"[2], helped them to cross the Red Sea on dry ground, turned bitter water into sweet, gave bread from heaven and so on. Moses had many tough times with the people. He had to intervene in their quarrels; he had to plea for them when God was angry with them because of their unfaithfulness.[3] It took forty years to travel through the wilderness of Sinai. At the end of the journey they reached Moab and there before they could reach their destination, which is the land of Canaan Moses dies.[4] In getting the people out of Egypt and leading them through the wilderness and in keeping them together as a people in spite of so many instances of fight and divisions, Moses proves himself to be a very able leader and manager. The process through which Moses liberated the people can be understood as an organised process comparable to the working of an organisation. This process of liberation, let us call, the Exodus Movement. Moses' approach was very much like the Seven-S approach of McKenzie Company. We can identify all the steps of the Seven-S approach in Moses' leadership. At the same time it was a leadership that transcends the Seven-S approach. We will explain Moses' approach first by identifying the seven steps and then point out the aspects of his leadership, which transcends the McKenzie method.

Strategy

In the seven-S approach strategy is the first. Applying it to Moses let us ask "what is the strategy of Moses?" By strategy is meant the final goal to be achieved through the various steps taken as means. It seems that we can identify the strategy of Moses as the formation of the people of God. In other words the Israelites who are now slaves to a foreign ruler are to be changed into a people of God. All that Moses does is in view of achieving this goal. That forming into a people of God is the ultimate strategy is clear in the mission of Moses. When he is called and sent to Egypt God says, "I will be with you; and this shall be the sign for you that it is I who sent you: when you have brought the people out of Egypt, you shall worship God on this mountain."[5] So worshipping God is the aim of liberation. Further, God asks Moses to repeat His words to Pharaoh. The words are:

> Thus says the LORD: Israel is my firstborn son. I said to you, "Let my son go that he may worship me." But you refused to let him go; now I will kill your firstborn son.[6]

So it is clear that being the Son of God is the state of being by which the Israelites define themselves. As sons of God they serve Him by worshipping. Therefore worshipping is not the ultimate aim rather being the people of God is the aim and that is the strategy of Moses.

Structure

The structure of the Exodus Movement may be explained as follows:

In the previous section of this dissertation we identified strategy as the formation of the people of God. For the realisation of the people of God Moses makes use of a definite structure. It consists of:

1. Getting the people out of Egypt.
2. Mediating a covenant between God and the people by means of which these people who were slaves will become a free people in an intimate relationship with God.
3. The preservation of the status as the people of God through a religious and social system.

Getting the People Out of Egypt

This is the first item in the structure of the Exodus Movement and the first step in making the non-people, a people and changing slaves of men into people of God. As we read through the pages of the Bible, especially chapters 2 to 30 of the Book of Exodus, we get an idea of what getting out of Egypt meant in the life of Moses. The immediate steps which Moses needed to take up are:

— Conscientise the people about the seriousness of the situation in which they are;

— Instil a sense of unity in the minds of the people;

— Reawaken their nostalgic attachment to their ancestors like Abraham, Isaac and Jacob;

— Encourage them to withstand temporary difficulties in view of permanent freedom and prosperity;

— Instil in them a hatred for slavery and a desire for freedom.

These are the things, which Moses had to do in relation to the people of Israel who were now slaves in Egypt. On the other side of the spectrum there was the need to subdue Pharaoh, the oppressor. We will take up each of these steps through which Moses realised of the first item of the structure namely getting the people out of slavery.

To explain these different steps for the realisation of the first item namely getting out of Egypt, Moses had first to change the people in such a way that they would be conscious of the seriousness of the situation. This is clear from the reaction of the people when Pharaoh denied them straw and demanded the same number of bricks to be made.[7] The people come to Moses and Aaron and say, "The LORD look upon you and judge! You have brought us into bad odour with Pharaoh and his officials, and have put a sword in their hand to kill us."[8] Though they are slaves and are mistreated by Pharaoh and the taskmasters the people are not conscious of the seriousness of the situation. They prefer putting up with the slavish situation than suffer any inconvenience for getting freedom.

Secondly there was no sense of unity among the people. This is clear in Exodus 2: 11-15. As the story goes, Moses sees two Israelites fighting with each other. When Moses tried to stop them the reaction of the people was, "Who made you a ruler and a judge over us?"

Thirdly as a result of their long stay in Egypt and in a different cultural milieu alienated from their ancestral land and culture, the people of Israel had almost forgotten who they were. This people can be brought out as a people only if they are able to rediscover their roots. For that Moses had to convince them that it was God of their ancestors that sent him to them. When God commissions Moses as his messenger and liberator of the people, God qualifies himself as "God of your Father, the God of Abraham, the God of Isaac and the God of Jacob."[9] This long identification of God as the God of the ancestors was meant to instil a nostalgic love in the people for their ancestral heritage. The people have to be conscious that they are one people, one family, brothers and sisters to each other and sons of the same father. Only this feeling and self-awareness will keep them together and encourage them to take up steps for liberation from Egypt.

Furthermore, the people were morally weak. They were not able to withstand difficulties. This may be due to the long years of slavery to the Egyptians. They went after insignificant and immediate gains forsaking permanent and valuable gains. A very important instance, which shows this mentality of the people, is given in Exodus 15: 22ff. When the people had no water in the wilderness they turn against Moses. They were ready to go back than suffer the inconvenience. Another instance of such an attitude of the people is in Exodus 16: 2ff. They had no food to eat and the reaction of the people was:

> If only we had died by the hand of the LORD in the land of Egypt, when we sat by the fleshpots and ate our fill of bread; for you have brought us out into this wilderness to kill this whole assembly with hunger.[10]

Moses had to conscientise the people before anything could be done to liberate them.

If the people themselves had to be prepared for liberation, on the other side was Pharaoh who had to be totally changed to let the people go. The ten plagues, which Moses performed in Egypt, are steps through which Moses changed the mind of Pharaoh gradually making him at the end to request the people to go out.

Mediating a Covenant Between God and the People

In the structure of the Exodus Movement another important element is that Moses acts as the mediator for establishing a covenant between God and the people. It is done on their way to the wilderness when they reached the mountain of Sinai. The story is given in chapters 19 to 24 of the Book of Exodus. God calls Moses to the mountain and after a long stay of forty days and nights with God, Moses comes out and conveys the message of God to the people. He also wrote down the conditions of the covenant and ratified it by the two important rituals – a sacrifice to God with the blood of the victims poured on the altar and the people and a common meal on the top of the mountain in the presence of God.[11]

The Preservation of the Status as the People of God Through a Religious and Social System

The next element in the structure of the Exodus Movement is that Moses acts as the instrument for establishing a permanent social and religious system.[12] The people can remain as the people of God only if they continue their relationship with God and their relationship with one another intact by means of a system. The social stability and the religious stability are seen as two aspects of the same reality. In fact according to the precepts in the Pentateuch social obligations are part of their religious obligations. The same way the religious obligation becomes part of their social obligations. The idea is that they should become one people of God. To be one people they have to be socially organised with rights and obligations. To be one people of God their obligations, even the social ones, are to be related to their obligations to God. The Ten Commandments—Exodus chapters 20 to 23 and the explanations of the Ten Commandments distributed all through the Pentateuch are at the same time rules governing social life and religious life. An analysis of the Ten Commandments will make this point clear.

The first three commandments are openly directed towards God. "You shall have no other gods before me", "You shall not make for yourself an idol, whether in the form of anything that is in heaven above, or that is on the earth beneath, or that is in the water under the earth. You shall not bow down to them or worship them; for I the LORD your God am a jealous God, punishing children for the iniquity of parents, to the third and the fourth generation of those who reject me, but showing steadfast love to the thousandth generation of those who love me and keep my commandments"[13]. This is the first commandment and it demands unalloyed devotion to God.

The second one prohibits wrongful use of the name of God.[14] The third commandment asks Sabbath observance spending the day for no work than to worship God.[15] These laws, which govern the relationship between God and the people, are later codified into a religious system with sacred objects and festivals. For any religion such things are necessary. There are certain sacred objects and sacred times, which are dedicated for the worship of God. In Exodus 25 we have the beginning of how the Jewish religion took shape with sacred objects and festivals. God asks Moses to make the Ark of the Covenant.[16] The Ark is the most important sacred object in the religion of the Jewish people. Around and in association with this most important sacred object other things are required. The Table for the Bread of the presence[17], the Lampstand[18], the Tabernacle with curtains[19], the Framework[20], the Curtain[21] etc are other objects related to the Ark of the Covenant, which is the most important sacred object and from which God will be communing with the people.[22]

In the Ten Commandments the rest of the laws govern social life. Respect for the parents, avoidance of theft, false witness, sexual offence, murder, coveting others' property etc are all rules that regulate social life. These seven rules are later expanded into a whole social system in the Book of Leviticus. But these two (the religious obligations and the social obligations) are inter-related. Offences against social obligations are understood as offences against God Himself. Thus through the mediation of Moses the people are formed into one people of God. This is the structure of the Exodus Movement.

System

The Exodus Movement was only the beginning of a process by which the people of Israel were made into a strong people politically well established and religiously well defined. "It developed unevenly, underwent change, and incorporated tension and conflict."[23] But in the time of Moses they were only moving into the future, which establish the system. Therefore, it is very difficult to speak of a system in the time of Moses. At the same time what Moses did and achieved are intimately inter-connected. If we want to see the leadership of Moses in terms of a system we can explain it as follows:

Moses evolved a system which was in tune with his mission. On the top of the system is the revealing God. He reveals His mind and plan about the people. The plan is the establishment of Israel as the people of God. This plan of God is revealed to Moses who acts as intermediary between God and the people. Moses receives the revelation from God and communicates it to the people—in the beginning to Pharaoh because liberation was dependant on his decision and later to the people themselves. There is also the role of Aaron. In the beginning Aaron was given to Moses as his assistant with important responsibilities. God says, "He (Aaron) indeed shall speak for you to the people; he shall serve as a mouth for you, and you shall serve as God for him."[24] But later Aaron's role is slowly reduced to a priestly role. Therefore the system has three inter-related parts in it. On the top is the eternal plan of God and at the other end or the lowest end is the people (including Pharaoh) to whom the plan of God is communicated and in between the two extremes is placed Moses with Aaron his assistant. These three factors are very intimately inter-related. God speaks not to the people directly, but to Moses and he is the one who communicates God's plan to the people. Yet we have to keep in mind a very important distinction between this system and the ordinary systems in our organisations and firms. It is not because God is not able to communicate directly with the people that He employs Moses as an intermediary. Yet in actual fact God does not directly speak with the people. So a system is maintained.

Style

Moses' style of functioning is very different from the functioning of any leader in an ordinary organisation. First of all in Moses' time the people were not organised into a nation, but only in the process of being formed into such a status. Therefore, the styles, which are used in ordinary organisations or firms, could not be used in the liberation movement led by Moses. He changes his style from time to time depending on the needs and contexts. In his relationship with God we can see clear consistency especially after he took charge of the mission entrusted to him. In his relationship with God he was almost like a doll in the hands of a child. Whatever God commanded he executed exactly. For the people Moses was in the position of God. Already in the scene of the commissioning God hints at it about the role of Aaron and Moses. God says, "He (Aaron) indeed shall speak for you to the people; he shall serve as a mouth for you, and you shall serve as God for him."[25] In other words, Moses was the visible form of God, who, invisibly guided and directed every movement within the organisation. Yet Moses was not just like a doll. Sometimes he intercedes for the people and makes demands on God, rather than just execute His word. An excellent example for this corrective attitude of Moses is found when God was enraged by the idolatry of the people.[26] Moses implores before the LORD saying, "O LORD, why does your wrath burn hot against your people, whom you brought out of the land of Egypt with great power and with a mighty hand? ... Turn from your fierce wrath; change your mind and do not bring disaster on your people."[27] The result of this prayer was that, "The LORD changed his mind about the disaster that he planned to bring on his people."[28] Therefore, it seems Moses' relationship with God had a double orientation in it. He was totally obedient and he exactly executed the plans of God. At the same time he was the leader of the people not just an ambassador of God. His leadership influenced his relationship with God in such a way that at sometimes he had to pacify the wrath of God.

Now what was his style within the organisation? Since he was in the position of God he could act only authoritatively because God acts authoritatively since he is the authority of everything. This authoritative style of Moses is seen all through his dealings with the people. He gives commands and they are obeyed. About what is to be done in connection with the celebration of the Passover, the journey from Egypt, the journey through the wilderness, the directives about the making of the Ark, the ordination of the priests etc are commanded by Moses and they are all done accordingly. Thus we have the picture of an autocrat or an authoritative leader in Moses. But these laws and regulations are not Moses' personal laws or regulations. Rather he simply communicates the mind of God and sees them executed exactly as God commanded. Therefore, the source of the authority or autocracy is God and not Moses. "Mosaic authority may be understood then, out of his participation in the power of God. ... The strength of that authority resides, then, in the power of God at the basis of his leadership."[29] At the same time when the people worshipped the golden calf Moses acts in a very extra ordinary way. He burns the idol in fire and dissolves it in water and makes the people drink it. Afterwards he commands the sons of Aaron to punish those who violated fidelity to God to the extent of killing three thousand people that day.[30] From every human standard this is a most authoritative and autocratic action. How to justify it? We can understand it only against the consuming anger of God. The idolatry had completely alienated the people from God and God separates Moses and the people telling him, "Now let me alone, so that my wrath may burn hot against them and I may consume them; and of you I will make a great nation."[31] The meaning of the divine words is that God is going to consume every idolater and Moses alone will be spared. It is in this context that Moses does this autocratic and authoritative action. The principle applied here is the death of a few to ward off total annihilation of the people.

If these steps were to ward off the total annihilation of people what is the name that is suited to this style? It is not autocratic, neither it is authoritative style. Rather the only name suited to it from the Seven-S approach is paternalism. It is a small punishment, which is of a medicinal nature. This is done first to instil fear of God in the minds of the people and make them repentant so that they may become more cautious in their future life. The paternal heart of Moses is clear in the subsequent prayer. When God saw that the people have rejected him and have gone after the idols the immediate reaction is a separation between the people and their leader Moses. God says, "Now let me alone, so that my wrath may burn hot against them and I may consume them."[32] So God has determined to put an end to the people of Israel. But God's reaction to Moses is quite different. Moses was not a partner in this sin. While the people were adoring the idol Moses was in close communion with God as God Himself had demanded. Therefore, God tells Moses, "Of you I will make a great nation."[33] This is the promise God had given to the fathers. To Abraham God had said, "I will make of you a great nation."[34] This promise to Abraham is repeated to Isaac, his son.[35] This promise is repeated in a dream to Jacob on his way to Paddanaram[36] and in another time when he was returning from Laban to his native land.[37] In these promises the land of Canaan was promised to the posterity of the ancestors, i.e., to the people of Israel. Now after the idol worship God is rejecting the people and making Moses alone the heir to the promises. "This was a magnificent opportunity for Moses to free himself from a people who shortly before had threatened to kill him when there was a shortage of water."[38] But the reaction of Moses is that the people should not be rejected. He goes up to God and prays, "Alas, this people has sinned a great sin; they have made for themselves gods of gold. But now if you will only forgive their sin—but if not, blot me out of the book that you have written."[39] Moses' reaction is just the opposite of God's reaction. He could very well be the heir to the inheritance and the people will be lost. But instead he prefers his ruin to the ruin of the people.[40] "He is not simply an instrument in the hands of an omnipotent God. ... Moses appeals to God to alter an announced intention on the basis of a prior promise."[41] This shows his fatherly attitude. Therefore, though there are certain occasions when Moses acts as an autocrat and authoritarian these are all to be understood as different means by which the people could be protected against total destruction. Therefore, the predominant style of Moses is to be understood as the paternalistic style.

We can notice other elements in Moses' style. For example he gives detailed direction in everything, which the people have to do. The whole movement depends on him after God. There is nothing, which he does not know. There is no point at which he had to consult others. There is no event directed by him, which ended in failure. From all these we can call his style of functioning as an expert style. But his expertise is not his own expertise. Rather his expertise is coming from his close communion with God. In Moses there is also another side. When his father-in-law gives him certain advice about lessening his responsibility by appointing seventy elders under him, he readily agrees it.[42] This was not consulting his father-in-law because he needs no consultation. He had clear directive from God. But he readily accepts a suggestion coming from a mature and experienced elderly man. It is a style comparable to the consultative or participatory style.

In short we can say Moses' style is a very complex style. It had different elements in it. Predominantly it was paternalistic. But he also made use of other styles to support and maintain the paternalistic style. The different styles used by Moses are shown in a diagram *(See Fig. 4.1 on next page)*. The diagram shows the different types of leadership styles adopted by Moses while leading the people from Egypt to Canaan. The important styles were authoritative, consultative, expert, and paternal. Though these were the different styles he adopted in accordance with the situations, an in-depth study reveals that among these styles paternal was his common style and so it is placed at the centre of the figure.

Staff

What is the staff or the human resource that is applied in the liberation movement led by Moses? If we take all persons and powers involved in the movement we can identify four levels of staff—God at the topmost position, Moses in close communion with God, Aaron who is Moses' assistant and spokesman, and the tribal leaders through whom Moses gives directives to the people and who accompany him on certain occasion to meet God on Mount Sinai. Thus Moses positions himself ideally and gets things done through right men under him. We will take each of these levels of staff and see how they function in this liberation movement.

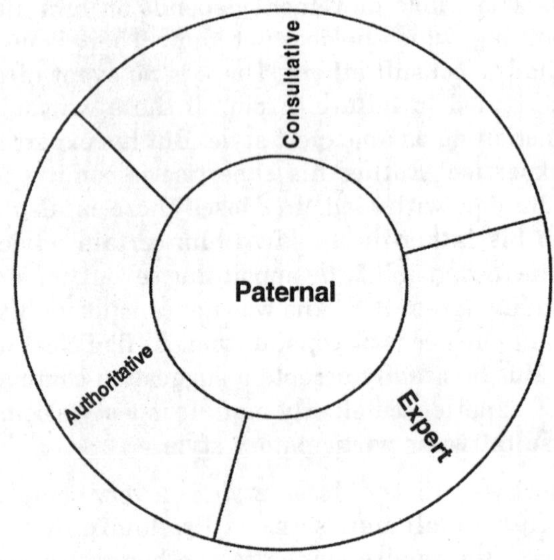

Fig. 4.1

Leadership Styles in the Moses' Movement of Liberation

God

The liberation movement is ultimately the work of God. It was God's decision to free the people from slavery to the Egyptians. In the scene of the commissioning of Moses God says, "I have observed the misery of my people who are in Egypt; I have heard their cry on account of their taskmasters. ... and I have come down to deliver them from the Egyptians, and to bring them up out of that land to…a land flowing with milk and honey…"[43] This plan of God is not a sudden decision when He was touched by the misery of the people. Rather it is only part of an eternally decided plan. In the covenant with Abraham God had already hinted at the destiny of Abraham's offspring and how God will deliver them. God speaks to Abraham, "Know this for certain that your offspring shall be aliens in a land that is not theirs, and shall be slaves there…and afterward they shall come out with great possessions."[44] What God is now doing is only the fulfilment of this prophecy and promise.

God is not only the remote planner of the liberation movement but also the one who directs every step and brings them into realisation. The ten plagues, which Moses performed in Egypt, are all the doings of God. He gives directions as to what to do and when to do and where to do as well as when to stop the plagues. The ritual of Passover, which the Israelites celebrated on the night of their deliverance, also was according to the directives of God. It is God who makes Pharaoh let the people go; it is God Himself who shows the direction, which the people should take; it is none other than God who intervenes on the way whenever there is any problem which the people face. Thus God stands at the top of this movement guiding and directing every detail of the movement.

Moses

After God it is Moses who takes on himself under God's directives, the responsibility of delivering the people. Moses' role is something unique having no parallel in other organisations and firms. Is he the manager? If managing is the duty of the manager Moses is, in a true sense the manager. But he is much more than a manager. He is like the owner and proprietor when a negative experience faces them and the way he intercedes with God to solve the problems gives us the impression that the whole movement is his own movement. This is because there is a two level identification in the life of Moses. As a true prophet and a servant of God his will is completely identified with the plan and desire of God. As a true Israelite, as one who loves his people Moses is totally identified with the people. It is this characteristic feature of the man that makes him unique in his role as leader, guide and manager.[45]

Aaron

The role of Aaron in the liberation movement is very unclear. To what shall we compare him in terms of the offices in the modern firms and organisations? Is he an assistant manager? A definite answer is difficult. In the beginning of the movement especially in dealing with Pharaoh, Aaron had a prominent role. Appointing Aaron as his spokesman solved the speech difficulty of Moses.[46] In Moses' dealing with Pharaoh, Aaron accompanies him. The same way when Moses speaks to the people Aaron is by the side. But later Aaron's role becomes more and more diminished. Just before giving the Ten Commandments Moses had a long interaction with God. He goes up to the mountain of Sinai and has close communion with God. But in that scene Aaron is not found. Only at the end of the encounter God asks Moses to bring Aaron with him.[47] In another scene which also is a scene of close communion with God Aaron is not found with Moses. But another person Joshua is brought to the presence of God and he is also qualified as Moses' assistant.[48] In another scene Aaron is found to be siding with the people against God and Moses. During the long encounter between God and Moses on mount Sinai under the cover of dense smoke and cloud Aaron makes a golden calf for the people to worship.[49] Though Aaron's involvement in this idolatrous worship is clear he is not punished. From the Old Testament standards it is strange that he is not punished. On another occasion he was "involved in a quarrel with Moses concerning Moses' cushite wife."[50] On this occasion also Aaron is not punished while Miriam who was his accomplice was punished.

It seems that Aaron's role is slowly being diverged from Moses' role. He began as an assistant of Moses. Later he was established as the high priest and his sons as priests.[51] This change of the role of Aaron is to be seen in conjunction with the development of the liberation movement as a simple deliverance from slavery to the establishment of a well-defined people. In the beginning the Israelites who went out from Egypt were not properly defined as a people. They had no laws pertaining to their social and religious life. But after the covenant with God at Sinai, they become a people, the people of God with rules and regulations governing the relationship among the people themselves and the relationship between the people and God. This transition brought in changes in the role of Aaron.

Seventy Elders

The elders are a group of people with certain responsibilities in the social and religious life of the people.

The Hebrew word for elders is *zaken* and it means elderly in age. The Hebrew word may be pointing to the origin of this class of people. Perhaps in the beginning age was the main criterion for selecting the elders. Anyway they "appear as a distinct social grade or collegiate body with distinct political or religious function."[52] We have two traditions concerning the role of elders in connection with the Liberation Movement of Moses. According to one tradition they were already elders among the people when Moses started the movement. In fact they were functioning as elders giving leadership to the people already in Egypt before Moses was sent as the liberator. In the scene of the commissioning God tells Moses, "Go and assemble the elders of Israel, and say to them, THE LORD, the God of your ancestors ... has appeared to me ..."[53] Here Moses is asked not to appoint elders but to assemble them. It shows that elders were already existing and they had some well-defined role within the society. But we do not know what exactly was their role before Moses started the Liberation Movement. In Exodus 15 we hear about certain Israelite supervisors who were beaten up by Pharaoh's taskmasters for not producing bricks as many as demanded by Pharaoh. Who are these people? They cannot be Egyptians. From the context it seems that taskmasters were Egyptians and the supervisors were Israelites themselves with leadership role among the Israelite slaves. It is these people who go to Pharaoh and complain against the rigidity of the demand.[54] Perhaps these supervisors were the same as the elders of the people. The new name supervisor was given to them in view of the role they played in the production of bricks. If our conclusion is correct, namely, that the elders and supervisors are the same we can say with some amount of certainty that the elders were representatives of the people and go-between for consultation with the king.

But after Moses had begun the movement we have another group of elders. They are chosen at the suggestion of Jethro, Moses' father-in law. About them we read, "So Moses listened to his father-in–law and did all that he had said. Moses chose able men from all Israel and appointed them as heads over the people, as officers over thousands, hundreds, fifties, and tens."[55] Their role also is clearly stated. Judging the people is their primary function. But they give their decision only on minor cases and they brought major cases to Moses for his decision.[56] From the mention that they were "chosen" it is clear that they are not the same as the already existing elders. Certain qualities are presupposed for the choice of these people. They are to be able men, men who fear God, trustworthy, who hate dishonest game etc.[57] In this context they are not called elders. Rather they are Judges of the people. We also do not know the number of these Judges. They are Judges over tens, fifties, hundreds, and thousands. Therefore, naturally we can guess that they were a large number. Further their grade is not the same. Those above ten people will be the lowest in the grade and those above thousand will be the highest.

There is another group of leaders. They are the seventy elders. They are with Moses and Aaron on Mount Sinai to encounter God on the mountain. They had a vision of God on the mountain and they ate and drank in the presence of God. They are qualified as "the chief men of the people of Israel."[58] This people cannot be the same as the judges appointed over tens, fifties, hundreds and thousands because here there is a definite number. They are only seventy. They share some of the privileges of Moses like seeing God face to face.

We have two other names in association with the encounter of God on the mountain. They are the names of Nadab and Abihu. Both are sons of Aaron. They are the rightful heirs to the priestly office of Aaron. They are on the mountain of God with Moses, Aaron and the seventy elders. They assist Aaron during the inauguration of his priestly ministry.[59] But afterwards they incense before the LORD without being commanded. As a result they were consumed by fire that came out from the LORD. Now what is their role in the community? It seems they were not simply priests, descendants of Aaron because all the sons of Aaron had the right to be priests and Aaron had other sons also. Moreover, these two go up to the mountain of the LORD, the other sons of Aaron are not given this privilege. On the mountain they are mentioned with the seventy elders. Did they have some privilege or position as special elders of the people? We do not know. Neither the Bible nor any other source is helpful to decide their position.

As Aaron's role changes from being the assistant of Moses to being the high priest, his sons also come to prominence as priests of the people. After the death of Nadab and Abihu, the remaining sons of Aaron Eleazar and Ithamar, become the priests of the people. Their function is essentially priestly function.

After the sons of Aaron who were heirs of Aaron's priesthood there is another class of people, the Levites whose duty also was associated with the temple and the liturgy. They are to assist Aaron. They are to do service at the tabernacle, furnish the tent of meeting. They are the possession of God as the first born of Israelite population.[60] But their position is below the position of priests and is assistants to the priests.

Another important office in Moses Liberation Movement is the one held by Miriam, the sister of Moses. After the crossing of the red sea she "led the women of Israel in song and dance", like the prophets of the ancient times.[61] She is designated as a prophetess.[62] But later she together with Aaron claimed equal status with Moses and was punished with leprosy.[63] Was her role integrated with the Liberation Movement? Or was it merely an unofficial and charismatic function? Nothing is certain.

We also read of certain spies who were sent by Moses to spy out the land of Canaan.[64] On another occasion some spies are sent to spy out Jazer.[65] The role of these people is not clear in the Bible. First of all we do not know if the spies in both cases are same persons. Secondly their role seems to be temporary. Except that they were given a duty on a particular occasion they had no permanent role to play in the Liberation Movement.

Over and above the persons and officers mentioned above we also read about people associated with the construction of the Ark of the Covenant. It is also called the tabernacle. These were skilled labourers chosen from among the people. Among them two names are important – Bezalel and Oholiab. According to Moses these two were "called by name by the LORD and were filled with the divine spirit" for undertaking the construction of the tabernacle and to teach others to be co-workers with them.[66] Though their role is important in the construction of the tabernacle they have no permanent position in the Liberation Movement or the organisation of the people for they are not permanent staff. They were called to do a work at a particular stage in the progress of the Movement.

The staff involved in the Liberation Movement are shown in the following diagram.

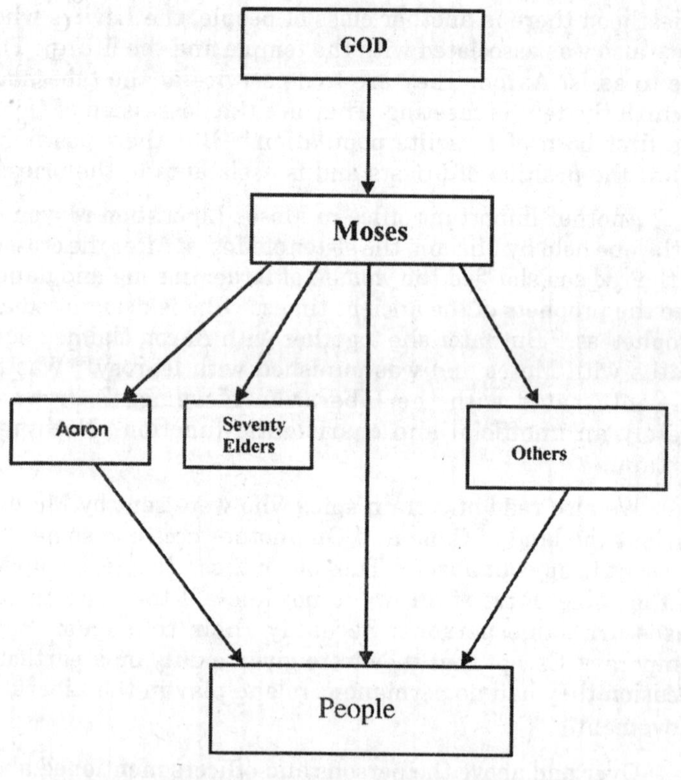

Fig. 4.2

The Staff in Moses' Liberation Movement

From the above diagram it is clear that in the liberation movement of Moses there are four levels of staff. God is the initiator and He reveals to Moses His intention to liberate the Israelites from the slavery of Pharaoh. Moses receives power and authority from God. God gives Moses even the minute details of each and every step at different stages of liberation movement. Aaron, the assistant and spokesman of Moses and seventy elders are the partakers in the authority of Moses. The category 'others' also receives direct communications from Moses. They are Jethro (Moses' father-in-law), Miriam (Moses' sister) etc. The liberation movement is a closed system and it is open only to Israelites. So the category "people" denotes the whole Israelites and they receive directions at times from Moses, then from Aaron, seventy elders and others. Thus the event of liberation movement becomes a success with the full support and co-operation from different levels of staff, though there are tensions at times, which Moses wins over with the help of God.

Shared Value

Shared value is the value that inspires all the people involved in an organisation, the value shared by the manager, the employees, the sales personnel etc. It is the common value and the force that keeps one attached to the organisation and inspires one to dedicate oneself for the welfare of the organisation. Now the question in the Liberation Movement of Moses is "what was the central value?" It seems liberty under God was the value shared by Moses, the people and all others involved in the Movement.[67] The people of Israel were slaves under Pharaoh. They were being tormented by the policies of the Egyptian rulers, policies meant for weakening them and keeping them always under Egyptian domination. The killing of the male children born to the Israelite women and very hard labour for keeping them always occupied with the work of the ruler were means by which the Pharaohs tried to perpetuate their slavery. It is to this people that Moses came with the message of liberation. They wanted to regain their liberty. But it was not a licentious freedom that they wanted; but liberty under God. It is not doing what the lower instincts of man dictated but doing things freely under the guidance of God. They wanted to be fully human beings with rights and obligations. Becoming fully human being is attaining liberty. On this point there was no disagreement among the people. Everybody wanted to be free and get out of the situation of slavery and this is the shared value of the Liberation Movement of Moses.

Even when we project liberty as the shared value we have to keep in mind the individual weakness of the people. There are cases of the people wanting to return to Egypt. But it is not because they did not like freedom but because they were not ready to pay the price for that. No value is attained without pain and pain is something that people detest. There are also cases of people quarrelling among themselves. This also is not proof that they did not share the value of liberty. Rather it is the result of a conflict between the common shared value and the value projected by the selfish nature of man.

Skills

When we speak of the skill that is used in an organisation we have first to make a distinction between skill and similar qualities like competence, talents and so on. A person attains competence through training and learning. Talents are qualities related to the personality of a person and are constant. On the other hand skill is not integrally related to training or learning, but are personal abilities of an individual. These abilities are used in particular situation either to solve a crisis or to boost a particular activity. With this basic idea of skill if we look at the Liberation Movement of Moses we can say that the fear of God is the skill applied throughout the movement. That is the ability with which all people involved in the movement tackle the situation. It is just the fear of God, which made Moses to take up the mission entrusted to him in spite of the fact that he was not an eloquent speaker. It is this fear of the LORD, which made the people honour him and also fear him and made them obey his commands.[68] Fear of the LORD is a concept that needs some explanation. It is not fear in the ordinary sense of the word. It is a technical expression in the Bible and it includes devotion to God and close relationship with Him

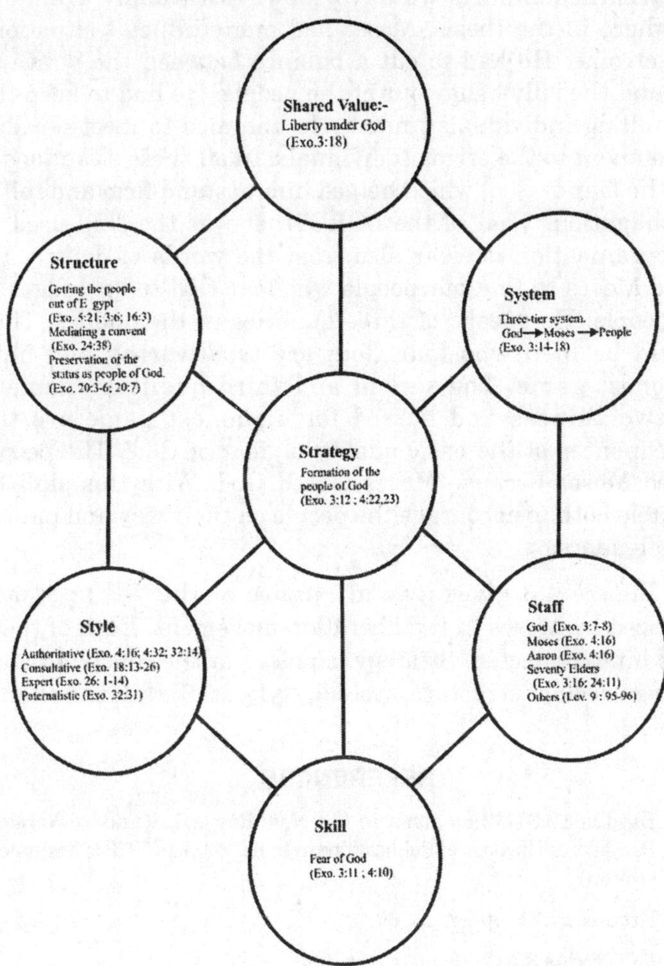

Fig. 4.3

7-S Approach in the Moses' Movement of Liberation

and a changed personality in consequence to the devotion and close relationship. As we have shown with many examples elsewhere in the thesis, Moses had many difficult situations to overcome. He had to cut a balance between the wrath of God and the silly behaviour of the people. He had to keep the quarrelling individuals united. He had also to meet out due punishment to the erring individuals. In all these situations it was the fear of God, which helped him to stand firm and fulfill his obligation. 'Fear of the LORD' that was the skill used in the organisation is clear also from the words of Jethro. He asked Moses to find out people who fear God to be Judges of the people. He speaks of three qualities in the Judges. They should be men who fear God, are trustworthy and hate dishonest game. The second and third qualities, namely, trustworthiness and hatred for dishonest game are the consequences of the basic quality of 'fear of God'. The people feared Moses because Moses feared God. With this skill he was able both to encourage the people on their way and punish the offenders.

Figure 4.3 gives a total picture of the 7-S approach practiced by Moses in the liberation movement. Each of these S's is interconnected. Strategy is placed at the centre because strategy decides structure, system, style, staff, skill and shared value.

REFERENCES

1. Exodus 12:31-32 as given in the New Revised Standard Version, Bangalore, Theological Publications in India, 2003, p. 59 (Old Testament section)
2. Exodus 13:21, op. cit., p. 60.
3. Cf. Exodus 33:12-23, op. cit., p. 80.
4. Cf. Deuteronomy 34, op. cit., pp. 191, 192.
5. Exodus 3:12, op. cit., p. 50.
6. Exodus 4:22, 23. op. cit., p. 51.
7. Cf. Exodus 5:1-21, op. cit., p. 52.
8. Exodus 5:21, op. cit., p. 52.
9. Exodus 3:6. op. cit, p. 50.

10. Exodus 16:3, op. cit., pp. 62-63.
11. Cf. Exodus 24:3-8, op. cit., p. 70.
12. Cf. Samuel J. Schultz, *The Gospel of Moses*, Moody Press, Chicago, 1979, p. 68.
13. Exodus 20:3-6, op. cit., p. 66.
14. Cf. Exodus 20:7, op. cit., p. 66.
15. Cf. Exodus 20:8-11, op. cit., p. 66.
16. Cf. Exodus 25:1-22, op. cit., Pp. 70-71.
17. Cf. Exodus 25:23-30, op. cit., p. 71.
18. Cf. Exodus 25: 31-39, op. cit., p. 71.
19. Cf. Exodus 26: 1-14, op. cit., p. 71-72.
20. Cf. Exodus 26: 15-30, op. cit., p. 72.
21. Cf. Exodus 26:31-37, op. cit., p. 72-73.
22. Cf. Exodus 25:22, op. cit., p. 71.
23. Norman K. Gottwald and Richard A. Horsley (editors), *The Bible and Liberation: Political and Social Hermeneutics*, Orbis Books, Maryknoll, New York, p. 143
24. Exodus 4:16, op. cit., p. 51.
25. Ibid.
26. Cf. Exodus 32, op. cit., pp. 78-79.
27. Exodus 32:11-12., op. cit., p. 78.
28. Exodus 32:14, op. cit., Pp. 78-79.
29. G.W. Coats, *The Moses Tradition*, JSOT Press, Sheffield, 1993, p. 75.
30. Cf. Exodus 32: 19-28, op. cit., p. 79.
31. Exodus 32:10, op. cit., p. 78.
32. Ibid.
33. Ibid.
34. Genesis 12:2, op. cit., p. 10.
35. Cf. Genesis 26:2-5, op. cit., p. 22.
36. Cf. Genesis 28:13-15, op. cit., p. 25.
37. Cf. Genesis 32:28-30, op. cit., p. 30.
38. C. Boff and G.V. Pixley, The Bible, the Church, and the Poor, Orbis Books, Mary Knoll, New York, 1986, p. 73.

39. Exodus 32:31, op. cit., p. 30.
40. Cf. G. W. Coats, The Moses Tradition, op. cit, p. 73.
41. G.W. Coats, *The Moses Tradition*, op. cit., p. 72.
42. Cf. Exodus 18:13-26, op. cit., p. 65.
43. Exodus 3:7-8, op. cit., p. 50.
44. Genesis 15:13-14, op. cit., p. 12.
45. Cf. C. Boff and G.V. Pixley, *The Bible, The Church, and the Poor*, Orbis Books, Mary Knoll, New York, 1986, p. 73.
46. Cf. Exodus 4:16, op. cit., p. 51.
47. Cf. Exodus 19:24, op. cit., p. 66.
48. Cf. Exodus 24:13, op. cit., p. 70.
49. Cf. Exodus 32, op. cit., pp. 78-79.
50. J.L. McKenzie, Dictionary of the Bible, London, Geoffrey Chapman, 1975, p. 1.
51. Cf. Leviticus 8:1-36, op. cit., pp. 94-95.
52. J.L. McKenzie, op. cit., p. 225.
53. Exodus 3:16, op. cit., p. 50.
54. Cf. Exodus 5:15-16, op. cit., p. 52.
55. Exodus 18: 24,25, op. cit., p. 65.
56. Cf. Exodus 18:26, op. cit., p. 65.
57. Cf. Exodus 18:21, op. cit., p. 65.
58. Exodus 24:11, op. cit., p. 70.
59. Cf. Leviticus Chapter 9, op. cit., pp. 95-96.
60. Cf. Numbers 3:5-13 op. cit., p. 119.
61. J. L. McKenzie, op. cit., p. 580.
62. Cf. Exodus 15:20, op. cit., p. 62.
63. Cf. Numbers 12:1-15, op. cit., p. 130.
64. Cf. Numbers 13:16-17, op. cit., p. 131.
65. Cf. Numbers 21:32, op. cit., p. 140.
66. Cf. Exodus 35:30-35, op. cit., p. 82.
67. Cf. Exodus 3:18, op. cit., p. 50.
68. Cf. Exodus 3:11, op. cit., p. 50.

5

Seven–S Approach in the Life of Jesus

In this chapter we examine the life of Jesus, the unparalleled leader of the New Testament. Jesus came as a liberator preaching a gospel of freedom. Jesus had a definite plan and purpose in his interactions with his contemporaries. In converting them to the ideals preached by him and in establishing a movement with the Apostles as the top-most leaders, Jesus acted as an able manager. Exploring the New Testament, we will, in this chapter, discuss how Jesus employed the Seven-S approach in his life.

Strategy of Jesus

To say anything about the strategy of Jesus we have first of all to identify the main goal in the life of Jesus. About the goal of Jesus there is no single idea in the New Testament. The sources, which may help us to identify the ultimate goal of Jesus, are the four Gospels. It is in them that we find Jesus' own words about himself, about his plan in life, about his strategy and so on. The other 23 books of the New Testament are expressions of individual writers about how the strategy of Jesus was being realised in particular communities. So in these books we have details of what the Christian Communities were doing or how these communities were formed. But they are not helpful to say what the overall strategy of Jesus was. This means we have to depend on the Gospels. Of course there are some stray expressions of the goal of Jesus in other parts of the New Testament also. For example, in 1 Thimothy 1:15 we read, "The saying is sure and worthy of full acceptance, that Christ Jesus came into the world to save sinners." This is an expression of the goal of the life of Jesus. But the author of this letter does not explain what "to save" means. Also we don't have any details about how Jesus realised this goal, i.e., his strategy for realising the goal. The concern of the author is to tell the people, especially the people of his community, how they should remain in the salvation brought by Jesus and experienced by them. All these mean that the Gospels are the only sources for a researcher of today to depend on for identifying and defining the strategy of Jesus.

In the Gospels we have marked difference about the life of Jesus from one Gospel to another. At the same time there is a generally agreed opinion among scholars that we can identify two main trends in the Gospel tradition. These are the traditions coming from the fourth Gospel (the Gospel according to John), which remain unique in many respects, not shared by any other of the Gospels. Secondly, there is the tradition that is inherent in the first 3 Gospels (Mathew, Mark and Luke). Though these three also differ in details they show a general agreement in terminology, theological perception and overall presentation of the goal of Jesus. This second tradition, since the passages in these Gospels can be put in parallel columns, is known as the synoptic tradition. In short we have mainly two traditions about Jesus. The synoptic tradition represented by the first three Gospels and the Johannine[1] tradition, which is found in the fourth Gospel.

In the synoptic tradition the goal of Jesus is expressed as bringing the *Kingdom of God*. This we can know from the first sermon of Jesus in Mark 1:14-15. The strategy of Jesus is clearly stated in the following words:

> Now after John was arrested, Jesus came to Galilee, proclaiming the good news of God, and saying, "The time is fulfilled, and the Kingdom of God has come near; repent, and believe in the good news."

This idea is also repeated so many times in that Gospel. The Greek original expression for Kingdom of God is *basileia tou theou*. There are a total of 15 occurrences of this expression in the Gospel of Mark. In the New Testament as a whole this expression occurs 67 times. This means it is a very important idea in the New Testament as a whole and in the synoptic tradition in particular.

In the Gospel of Mathew, which also shares the synoptic tradition there is the expression "Kingdom of heaven" which is more frequent than the expression Kingdom of God. In that Gospel Kingdom of heaven (*basileia tou uoranou*) occurs a total of 31 times while the expression "Kingdom of God" is found only 5 times. With a slight difference in nuance "Kingdom of heaven" means almost the same as "Kingdom of God."[2]

What does the Kingdom of God mean? In fact the Greek word *basileia* is a noun form derived from *basileus*, which means king. It means "*the state of being a king*" or "*kingship*". In ordinary use the English word kingdom is understood in a territorial sense. But that is not the meaning of the term in the Gospels. Rather it is a situation in which God becomes the king and ruler of the individuals and communities. Therefore, a better translation would be the kingship of God or the rule of God. In both cases it has nothing to do with territory. It has to do with the choice of the person or persons or the mental attitude of the individuals. It is accepting God as the ultimate ruler and guide of one's life.[3]

Luke has more detailed view about the kingship or rule of God. This is expressed in 4:16-19 of the Gospel. There it is said that as an inauguration of Jesus' ministry, Jesus went to a synagogue in Nazareth and chose a passage from the prophecy of Isaiah and read it aloud in the hearing of the congregation and then He proclaimed that this scripture passage had been fulfilled that day in their hearing. In other words Jesus is proclaiming that what Isaiah did speak about the Christ is now fulfilled in His person. The passage from Isaiah gives the details of what the Messiah is meant to be and what His goal of life would be. The passage is:

> The Spirit of the Lord is upon me, because he has anointed me to bring good news to the poor. He has sent me to proclaim release to the captives and recovery of sight to the blind, to let the oppressed go free, to proclaim the year of the Lord's favour.[4]

Since the proclamation comes at the beginning of Jesus' public ministry we should understand this as the Lucan version of the strategy of Jesus or at least as intimately connected with the strategy of Jesus. It is what Luke understands by the coming of the Kingdom of God.

Coming to the Gospel of John, we find there a different terminology and emphasis. In John the expression of Kingdom of God is very rare, though not completely absent. There are only 2 occurrences of the phrase in John (3:3 and 3:5). But he has another expression, which is parallel to this in meaning. The new expression is 'life' (*zoe*). This word occurs alone or in combination with the adjective *eternal*. But whether alone or in combination with the adjective *eternal* the expression means the same. Altogether *zoe* occurs 37 times in the Gospel. Giving life to the world, to His disciples, is Jesus' goal of life. The strategy of Jesus is expressed in clear terms in this Gospel in the following words. "I came that they may have life, and have it abundantly."[5]

This idea that Jesus came to give life is expressed in several other occasions also. For example in 1:4 we read "in him was *life*, and the *life* was the light of all people." The Evangelist, as a conclusion to his gospel, says that he wrote the gospel so that the readers may read it and believe in him "and that through believing you may have *life* in his name."[6] So we can say with confidence that the expression life, though it may have slight difference in emphasis and nuance, means the same as the kingdom of God in the synoptics. In short we can say that the strategy of Jesus was the establishment of the Kingdom of God.[7] Expressions vary slightly, but the idea is the same.

Jesus had a mission which was, 'the establishment of the Kingdom of God'. The strategy adopted was to convey the superiority of spiritualism over materialism and the dominance of eternal life. Creating a strong urge for eternity and salvation through the grace of God is seen throughout in his teachings and fellowships.

Structure

The structure of the Kingdom of God as conceived by Jesus is clearly stated in the Gospel of Mark. In the inaugural ceremony of Jesus this structure is clear. Accordingly, as Mark himself notes it, "Jesus came to Galilee proclaiming the good news of God, and saying, *The time is fulfilled, and the Kingdom of God has come near; repent, and believe in the good news.*"[8] The first part of the proclamation namely, "the time is fulfilled and Kingdom of God has come near" refers to the action of God. It is God who fulfils the time and brings the Kingdom of God near to man. Only God is able to do that. But the concrete realisation of the Kingdom of God is stated in the second part of the statement, which reads, "repent and believe in the good news". The second part needs certain explanation. Already we can notice that it has two aspects – one is repentance, the other is belief in the good news. How do we understand these two aspects of the Kingdom? The word repent is the translation of the Greek word *metanoeo*. It means to repent. In the New Testament this word in the verbal form and its noun form *metanoia* are very frequent. The verbal form occurs a total of 34 times and the noun form occurs a total of 24 times in the New Testament. *Metanoeo* is a compound word. In it we can identify two words, *meta* and *nous*. *Meta* means change, *nous* means mind. So *metanoeo* means change of mind or heart. So the proclamation of Jesus is an invitation to a change of heart. In fact the English word "*repent*" is too poor to express all the richness of the Greek expression. It is not simply "feeling sorry about a past action", which is the normal meaning of repentance.

But the Greek word *metanoeo* is a total change of heart. *Nous* (mind) is, according to the Greek thinking, the seat of all knowledge, feelings, likings, preferences and the like. So what Jesus demands is such a total change.[9] This is demanded of man; and this is one element in the Kingdom of God.

Secondly Jesus demands faith in the Gospel. In Jesus' own words, the demand is: "believe in the gospel or good news". What does this mean? It means believing and becoming good news. This demand of Jesus needs to be understood properly. First of all we have to know what gospel is. Secondly, we have to know what believing is. Thirdly we have to know what believing in the gospel is or how one can believe in the gospel. These are all terms and expressions that refer to the spiritual realm and they have to be properly understood. In the spiritual realm there is no counting as one, two, three or as now and then or as first and second. The spiritual realm is the realm of eternity, the realm of the constant and unchanging now. Therefore, we cannot split the demand for believing in the gospel as subject and object or as verb and object. Believe in the gospel means believe that you are gospel or believe that your life has become a gospel. To make a little clearer, it means believe that you experience the gospel in your life. We will come to this idea and explain what gospel is.

Gospel is the English translation of the Greek expression *euaggelion*. This is an expression, which has its origin in the Old Testament of the Bible. The verbal form of this word – *euagglisesthai* (to evangelise or make good news or proclaim good news) is found in the Greek translation of the prophecy of Isaiah.[10]

In Isaiah there is no occurrence of the noun form. It seems the noun form was coined by the Church of the New Testament times. The first use is by Paul in the first letter to the Thessalonians[11] (1 Thessalonians 1:5; 2:2; 2:4, 8, 9 and 3:2). It is possible that Mark has borrowed this expression from the tradition of the Church or from Paul in particular. Now what is the meaning of gospel? As we have seen it has an Old Testament background. It is bringing good news. It is, in other words, bringing a new experience in the life of the audience. When Jesus says "believe in the gospel", he means believe and experience a new situation in your lives. So believing is not about a situation but believing is making a new situation, is experiencing a new situation. Especially to be noted is the peculiar use of the word "believe" with its object the good news. It is not believing that you have a good news. Rather believe that you are good news. It means, in other words, belief and good news are not separate from each other. Believing is rather the experiencing of the good news.

To understand the importance of this demand let us move to the gospel of Luke. As we said above Jesus comes, reads the passage of Isaiah and tells that in their hearing that is fulfilled. We may understand the prophecy as a promise that God is sending a messenger who announces the good news. But the prophecy is not in the third person. The prophecy is in the first person. It is that "the Lord has sent me". So there is no question of fulfilling. So what are fulfilled are the other clauses in the proclamation namely release to the captives, recovery of sight to the blind, liberation to the oppressed and coming of the year of the Lord's favour. So these are the immediate result of believing or the effect of the coming of the Kingdom of God. That is why in the place of the Marcan proclamation of the good news Luke has a proclamation of these experiences. It means the good news is this experience. Believing in the good news is experiencing this new situation.

Thus two are the elements in the structure of Jesus' programme of life or the Kingdom of God. They are *repentance* or *metanoia* and the experience of a new situation in life, a situation of liberation from all sorts of bindings and captivities and the experience of freedom.[12]

System

In all ordinary Organisations there is a well defined system, that is, the different parts functioning together in an inter-related way so much so that no part of the system can be affected without effecting the other parts. Was there such a system in the functioning of Jesus? 'No' is the answer available from the pages of the New Testament. The main reason is that Jesus is much more than the owner or the manager of what was being done and achieved by Him. He was all in all and without Him nothing was possible. The same way with Him everything was possible with or without any other personnel in the movement or organisation. The fact is that Jesus started not an organisation as such, rather a Movement. But after the death and resurrection of Jesus, the Movement organised itself into a well defined system—with interdependent persons and functions. All this means that in the time of Jesus there was no system of the type we can think of in the life of the Christian Church or in any present day organisation. At the same time there are certain traits of Jesus' Movement, which could be developed into a system in the future. Anyway, the Movement in Jesus' time cannot be understood as anti system or non-system. It was a system in the process of being formed. How do we name that system? A naming is possible only after analysing some of the ways in which system nature was budding in that Movement.

While speaking about the strategy of Jesus we quoted Mark 1:14-15 as reflecting the strategy of the Movement. According to that passage Jesus came to Galilee and preached the good news saying, "The time is fulfilled, and the Kingdom of God has come near; repent, and believe in the good news."[13] And the next idea in the gospel is not that Jesus went on from place to place preaching the same message in the same terms or in similar terms. Rather the very next scene in the life of Jesus shown to us is His encounter with a few fishermen in the sea of Galilee. The Marcan gospel is very clear in making a distinction between the first preaching and His encounter with the fishermen. The text reads:

> As Jesus passed along the Sea of Galilee, he saw Simon and his brother Andrew casting a net into the Sea—for they were fishermen. And Jesus said to them, "Follow me and I will make you fish for people." And immediately they left their nets and followed him. As he went a little farther, he saw James son of Zebedee and his brother John, who

> were in their boat mending the nets. Immediately he called them; and they left their father Zebedee in the boat with the hired men, and followed him.[14]

The style of this passage is very different from that of Mark 1:14-15. There was a note of immediacy and urgency in the first preaching. It is said, "Jesus came to Galilee." But here it was "while Jesus was passing along". There is no preaching of any fulfilment or any invitation to repent or even to believe. Perhaps these people whom Jesus called to follow him were already believers. In other words in a former preaching these people had repented and believed. This is an invitation to a different thing. It is to follow Jesus. Are we not to sense the germination of a system nature in the movement of Jesus?

We have another instance of a similar event in the life of Jesus. That is in Mark 2:14. Almost the same terminology as 1:16-20 and almost the same style are detectable here also. It is the scene of the calling of a fifth disciple, Levi, by name. The text reads:

> As he was walking along, he saw Levi son of Alphaeus sitting at the tax booth, and he said to him, "Follow me." And he got up and followed him.

In both the scenes the calling happens "as Jesus was passing along or walking along." The words spoken to these men also are the same, "Follow me." In these scenes the invitation is not simply to repent and believe, but something else. Let us call it the germination of the system nature. In another part of the gospel we have reference to these men whom Jesus specially called. It is in the scene of the appointment of the Apostles. There we read:

> He went up the mountain and called to him those whom he wanted, and they came to him. And he appointed twelve, whom he also named apostles, to be with him, and to be sent out to proclaim the message, and to have authority to cast out demons.[15]

Certain things, which we have to note from the passage, are the following:

1. It is said, he called to him...and they came to him. It is the same terminology as the terminology used in the scene of the calling of the disciples (Mark. 1: 16-20). "He calls" and "they come"
2. Message is not to be preached to them unlike in Mark 1:15 rather they are elected to proclaim the message.
3. Also the word "appoint" is used about them, "And he appointed twelve."

From these observations it becomes clear that we have to distinguish between two things. One is the proclamation of the good news by Jesus. Second is the election of certain people to proclaim the good news. So in this stage, we can see three elements in the Movement. There is Jesus at the top as the primary proclaimer and within his authority there are others who also are appointed to proclaim the good news. There is also the function of the Movement, which is the proclamation of the good news. Then there are the common people who are the beneficiaries to whom the good news are proclaimed and who are brought to repentance and belief.

In the gospel of Luke we have another scene of how the Movement was taking a system shape. The text reads:

Soon afterwards he went on through cities and villages, proclaiming and bringing the good news of the Kingdom of God. The twelve were with him, as well as some women who had been cured of evil spirits and infirmities: Mary, called Magdalene, from whom seven demons had gone out, and Joanna, the wife of Herod's steward Chuza, and Susanna, and many others, who provided for them out of their resources.[16]

This passage sheds light to another face in the system-taking development of the Movement of Jesus. Still it is a Movement in the very literal sense itself. Jesus is moving from place to place. But it is also a system where Jesus is shown at the centre of the system surrounded by the twelve apostles who are themselves assisted by a few women disciples who were converted, healed and freed by Jesus. It is a circular shape of the Movement of Jesus. There is also the idea of the inter-dependence of the different factors, which make up the circle. Jesus is shown as the central power and inspiration. But to some extent he needs the assistance of others. He is assisted by the twelve. What exactly was the assistance given by the disciples is not clear in the text. It is said that they were with him. Then there are the women who are clearly designated as assistants. It is they who provide for Jesus and the disciples out of their resources. The position and the type of assistance, which the apostles were rendering becomes clear in Luke 9: 1-2 where we read: "Then Jesus called the twelve together and gave them power and authority over all demons and to cure diseases, and he sent them out to proclaim the Kingdom of God and to heal."

So doing the same work as Jesus did was, it seems, the function of the apostles.

A more detailed picture of the system nature of the Movement we get from Luke 10: 1 where we read: "After this the Lord appointed seventy others and sent them on ahead of him in pairs to every town and place where he himself intended to go."

Who are these seventy? So far there is no mention of the seventy. They come to the scene without any mention earlier. Could they be 'many others' of Luke 8: 3? From a strict linguistic point of view we have to say that they cannot be those many others because there in Luke 8: 3 the word is feminine plural (*eterai pollai* – many others) while in Luke 10: 1 the noun is masculine plural (*eterous* – others). Yet there is no reason to doubt that there were women also in the seventy who were sent by Jesus and these women could be those who are mentioned as "many others" in Luke 8: 3.

From all these observations we can say the following about the system nature of the Movement. It was only slowly that the Movement took a system shape. In the first place we have only Jesus, single-handed, proclaiming the good news. Slowly certain disciples are called who were meant for being sent by him to proclaim the good news. Then there are certain others who were also being trained by Jesus. But about this group and their training we have no reference in the gospel. This people also assist Jesus as preachers. Then there is a group of women who provide for Jesus and the disciples. It is a mobile system as we read from Luke 8: 1, moving from town to town and from village to village. It was not founded on a particular place or an office. But it has some sort of an inter-dependant existence and in that sense it was being shaped into a system. What name shall we give it? Let us call it a '**mobile system**' or '**ever moving system**' that aspires for eternal life.

Style

Style is the next factor in the 7-S approach to management. We have given a definition of style and the different forms of styles practised in organisations. Now can we speak of a style in the functioning of Jesus? If so what is the specific nature of that style?

Every functioning has a style. Though it may differ from function to function and organisation to organisation. In the case of Jesus also we have to speak of a style. But what type of style was it? Jesus went about preaching the good news and healing the people and freeing them from the possession of demons. Jesus was the only authoritative and irreplaceable factor in that movement. That means everything depended on him and without him the system could not continue. Jesus' style of functioning evokes admiration in the minds of the people. It is reported about the reaction of the people, that "they were all amazed and glorified God, saying, 'We have never seen anything like this!'"[17] Also about the preaching and healing of Jesus it is reported, "What is this? A new teaching – with authority! He commands even the unclean spirit, and they obey him."[18] From these can we say that Jesus' style was autocratic or authoritative style? It does not seem to be. The same Jesus who commands the demons to depart from the people[19] and who heals people with a word or a gesture like taking the sick by the hand[20] is also very compassionate and he mingles with people in a very friendly way. About his healing a leper it is said, "Moved with pity, Jesus stretched out his hand and touched him, and said to him, "I do choose. Be made clean!'"[21] In another scene we see Jesus function with some sort of magnetic power. The disciples were called and immediately they left everything and followed him.[22] We have also another instance where the fatherly heart of Jesus is well expressed. When a paralytic was brought to him Jesus says, "Son, your sins are forgiven." Towards the end of Jesus' life in the world we have many scenes of controversy between himself and Jewish leaders. There Jesus uses very strong words to condemn the hypocratic attitude of the leaders. For example in Mathew 23: 13-36 we have a long series of condemnation of the Jewish leaders. Jesus says, "Woe to you, Scribes and Pharisees, hypocrites!" He qualifies them as hypocrites, blind guides, blind fools, white washed tombs, snakes and so on. So in this passage we have an outburst of very angry words. Should we not in the light of this language qualify Jesus an autocrat? But immediately after this controversy as conclusion to it we see Jesus as very sympathetic and almost at the point of weeping about the fate of Jerusalem.

> Jerusalem, Jerusalem ...how often have I desired to gather your children together as a hen gathers her brood under her wings, and you were not willing...for I tell you, you will not see me again until you say, 'Blessed is the one who comes in the name of the Lord.'"[23]

There is another face of Jesus' style of functioning. It is consultative style. In the second miracle of the multiplication of bread Jesus first consults the disciples. It is said, "Jesus called his disciples and said to them, 'I have compassion for the crowd, because they have been with me now for three days and have nothing to eat.'"[24] Jesus is consulting the disciples about the course of action to be taken to relieve the tension of the situation.

The transformational leadership style is another important style in Jesus' functioning. The specific characteristics of this style are that it ignites the spark of power, faith, and love in those who are touched by such leaders. In fact transformation takes place internally. But its impulses are visible outside. Jesus is a wonderful motivator who with his one word or action wins the heart of others. There are a number of such examples that we can quote from the pages of the New Testament of the

Bible. On his way to Jericho Jesus happens to meet Zacchaeus, a short fellow who was on a sycomore tree to see Jesus. Though he never intend to be seen by anybody, Jesus called him by name and told him that he is going to be his guest that day. This very action of Jesus transformed the life of Zacchaeus and in the middle of the dinner he stood up and said to Jesus, "Look, half of my possessions, Lord, I will give to the poor; and if I have defrauded anyone of anything, I will pay back four times as much."[25] John in his Gospel has also narrated an event wherein Jesus makes a long conversation with a Samaritan woman, who has been a sinner. At the end of the conversation we see that she recognises Jesus as the Messiah and through her many of the Samaritans believed in Jesus.[26]

We have another window to the style of Jesus and it is in his own words. It was in the context of the mother of the two of the disciples requesting first and second positions for her sons in Jesus' Kingdom. Jesus not only refuses to give any guarantee for such positions but give instructions as to the right attitude his disciples should have. He compares offices in his Movement with offices in other organisations. He says,

> You know that the rulers of the gentiles lord it over them, and their great ones are tyrants over them. It will not be so among you; but whoever wishes to be great among you must be your servant and whoever wishes to be first among you must be your slave.[27]

After this instruction Jesus points to himself as the model for them to imitate. There he says, "Just as the Son of Man came not to be served but to serve, and to give his life a ransom for many."[28] So here the style is a servant style.

We have seen many aspects of the style of functioning of Jesus. There is authority, compassion, consultation, servant like attitude, severe criticism, fatherly concern etc. That means Jesus' style is a mixed style and no simple name is possible. Yet the fatherly concern is the dominant attitude. Even when he criticises the Jewish officials it is out of compassion for them and sorrow at their inability to be converted. Therefore it is a many faceted style. What name shall we use for it? Let us call it a 'family style' because in the family the father has compassion, he shows authority, comes down on children with criticism, but never puts them down. Father always, the ideal father at least desires the good of the family members. Therefore, let us qualify the style of Jesus as the **'family style'**.

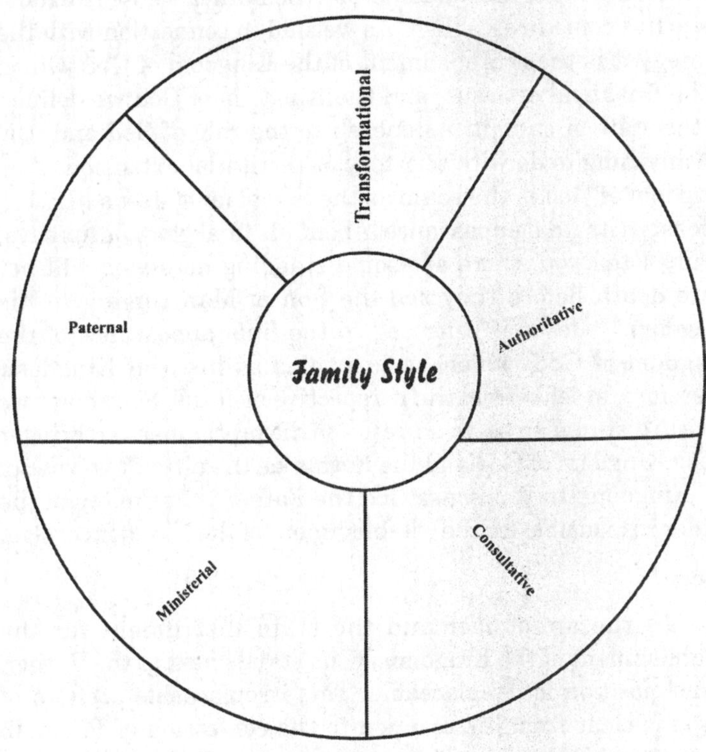

Fig. 5.1

Leadership Styles in the Jesus Movement

The diagram gives a clear picture of the different leadership styles practiced by Jesus in His approach with the people. Though the styles are different in different situations the core of His styles seems to be *family style* and so it is kept at the centre of the diagram.

Staff

In Jesus' Movement there are different persons functioning as staff in different levels of responsibility. They are:

God

On the top of the ladder is God the Father whose Kingdom Jesus has come to establish. As we said in connection with the strategy it is the establishment of the Kingdom of God, which is the final goal of Jesus, and the Kingdom of God we defined as the state of submitting oneself to the rule of God and it is not anything to do with territory or territorial extension. This Kingdom of God is the same as the Kingdom of Jesus himself, at least in its final appearance. About his final glory Jesus says, "Truly I tell you, there are some standing here who will not taste death before they see the Son of Man coming in his Kingdom."[29] Jesus is referring to the final appearance of the Kingdom of God, which he identifies as his own Kingdom. Therefore, at least from the perspective of Jesus' Movement we have to distinguish between Jesus as the proclaimer and bringer of the Kingdom of God and the Father as the ultimate owner of the Kingdom. In this sense God the Father is at the top of the ladder responsible for the establishment of the Kingdom of God.

Jesus

As the announcer and the main instrument for the establishment of the Kingdom Jesus stands next to the Father. Jesus' position is irreplaceable. This irreplaceable position of Jesus is clear from his reaction to the confession of Peter. To the question, "But who do you say that I am?" Peter answered by saying, "You are the Messiah (Christ), the Son of the living God." To this confession of faith Jesus reacts by promising him the keys of the Kingdom of Heaven.[30] Thus confession of faith in Jesus becomes very important in the Kingdom of God. We can refer to another instance in the life of Jesus. When an epileptic was brought to him, Jesus blames their faithlessness and says, "You faithless and perverse generation, how much longer must I be with you? How much longer must I put up with you?"[31] Here it is clear that Jesus is the one who brings the Kingdom of God into realisation. In his controversy with the Jews Jesus says, "See your house is left to you, desolate. For I tell you, you will not see me again until you say, "Blessed is the one who comes in the name of the Lord."[32] Here also the establishment of the House of God (the Kingdom of God) is intimately related with the confession of faith in Jesus. Thus Jesus is not only the bringer of Good News of the Kingdom of God but also part and parcel of the content of the Kingdom.

Twelve Apostles

After Jesus the twelve apostles form the next group of persons in the staff of Jesus' Movement. At the very beginning of the election of the apostles Mark says,

> He went up the mountain and called to him those whom he wanted, and they came to him. And he appointed twelve, whom he also named apostles, to be with him, and to be sent out to proclaim the message, and to have authority to cast out demons.[33]

Four expressions in this report need special explanation. Jesus called to him, "whom he wanted." The Greek word translated as "wanted" is *thelo*. It refers to the free and personal liking of Jesus. The appointment of the apostles was a totally free act. It was not on the basis of any qualification on the part of the apostles. Rather it is a free choice. We will comment more about it when we come to the different approaches to the staff. Here it suffices to say that the appointment was a free act from the part of Jesus. That means there was nothing that made necessary and inevitable to appoint them.

"To be with him"

The first function of the apostles seems to be the companionship of Jesus. They have to be with him. What does 'being with' mean? First of all we may think of their accompanying Jesus in his missions. After the appointment of the twelve almost invariably they are with Jesus in all his missions. Immediately after the appointment of the twelve we read, "Then he went home and the crowd came together again, so that they could not even eat. When his family heard it, they went out to restrain him..."[34] Who are these "they"? And what is meant by "home"? The home cannot be the house of Mary and Joseph because in the next verse we read that his family went out to restrain him. Therefore, the home would be some house in which Jesus and the disciples retired after their work. The same way the "they" could be understood as Jesus and the twelve. The twelve are seen as asking clarification for the parable of the sower.[35] In Mark 4: 34 we are told that after speaking in parables Jesus used to explain "everything in private to the disciples." After that Jesus invites the disciples to go to the other side of the sea of Galilee. In Mark 6:1 we read, "He left that place and came to his hometown, and his disciples followed him." "Being with" means accompanying Jesus in his mission and staying with him. This may be understood as the period of training for the disciples. Training means not simply the practical know-how but also a deeper knowledge of the reality of the Kingdom of God, a spiritual awareness and closeness with the realm of the divine. Secondly it means practical training and acquiring sufficient know-how of preaching the Gospel and dealing with people and solving their spiritual and physical problems.

To be sent out

This phrase may refer to the mission of the disciples. In the synoptic gospel, especially in Mathew and Luke, we have two phases of the mission of the disciples – one in the lifetime of Jesus and another after the resurrection. In the first phase of their mission they were asked to remain within the territory of the Jewish people. They were not allowed to go to the areas inhabited by the Samaritans or the Gentiles.[36] In the second phase of their mission (i.e., after the resurrection of Jesus) there is a universal widening of the scope of the mission. About this phase we read as follows:

> Jesus came and said to them, "All authority in heaven and on earth has been given to me. Go therefore and make disciples of all nations, baptizing them in the name of the Father and of the Son and of the Holy Spirit and teaching them to obey everything that I have commanded you."[37]

To have authority to cast out demons

This is the fourth characteristic of the appointment of the twelve. In the beginning we see Jesus as the sole authority to cast out demons. But after their appointment they share in Jesus' authority. About the first phase of their mission we read, "So they went out and proclaimed that all should repent. They cast out many demons ..."[38] So it is no more Jesus alone who has the authority to cast out demons. The disciples share this authority. Yet we don't see them as having the same measure of the authority. There are cases, which they are not able to solve. We hear about the father of an epileptic boy that though he brought his son to Jesus' disciples they were not able to cure him.[39] Anyway a share of the authority of Jesus over the evil spirits is given to the disciples.

The Seventy Disciples

They are the next members of the staff. About this category we read only in the gospel of Luke.[40] Their mission is almost the same as that of the twelve. Yet their authority seems to be limited. First of all their mission is just to prepare the people to receive Jesus when he himself will be approaching them. About their appointment we read that he "sent them on ahead of him in pairs to every town and place where he himself intended to go."[41] This means they have no independent authority. Their mission is only a preparatory mission. They are meant to prepare the way for Jesus. The same way they are asked only to preach and to heal the sick. But casting out demons is not included in their authority. Did they have a mission after the resurrection of Jesus? It seems they also shared the second phase of the mission of the twelve. When Jesus appeared to the disciples after his resurrection there were not only the twelve in the group, but also others, especially the two disciples—they are not members of the twelve - who went to Emmaus were with them.[42] On the day of Pentecost when Jesus empowered his disciples to be sent out on their mission with the outpouring of the Holy Spirit there were many in the group to receive the Holy Spirit, both men and women.[43] Therefore it is clear that the seventy were given a second phase of the mission to all the nations.

The Women

"The women who followed Jesus before and after his death played a full part in the proclamation of the prophetic message of Jesus. ...In the Jesus' movement the women were clearly and without question partners of the men."[44] Already we have seen that certain women were with Jesus helping him in his mission.[45] What is the nature of their mission is not clear. May be they were helping Jesus and the disciples with their material possessions.[46] Whatsoever be the nature of their work they also share the second phase of the mission because they are seen with the other disciples on the day of Pentecost.[47] According to the gospel of John, it seems the women shared also the mission of proclaiming Jesus. We have at least one example in the person of the Samaritan women. After her encounter with Jesus and conversion through his words she goes out to her people and says, "Come and see a man who told me everything I have ever done! He cannot be the Messiah, can he?"[48] The result of this proclamation was that "They left the city and were on their way to him."[49] Therefore at least from the example of the Samaritan woman we have to think that the women disciples also shared the responsibility of proclaiming Jesus. Another example is Mary of Magdalene. After his resurrection Jesus sends her away with the words, "Go to my brothers and say to them, 'I am ascending to my Father and your Father, to my God and your God."[50] As directed by Jesus she announces the resurrection of Jesus to the disciples.[51]

Thus we have different category of persons in the staff of Jesus' Movement. God the Father is on the topmost position. It is His Kingdom that Jesus came to establish. Next in the ladder is Jesus who is irreplaceable announcer and bringer of the Kingdom. Then we have the twelve apostles who share all the authorities of Jesus including the authority to cast out demons. In the next step are the seventy. They have all authorities except the one to cast out demons. After them stand the women who provide for Jesus and the disciples and also share in proclaiming Jesus in his earthly life and also after his resurrection. The staffs involved in Jesus' Movement are shown in the following diagram.

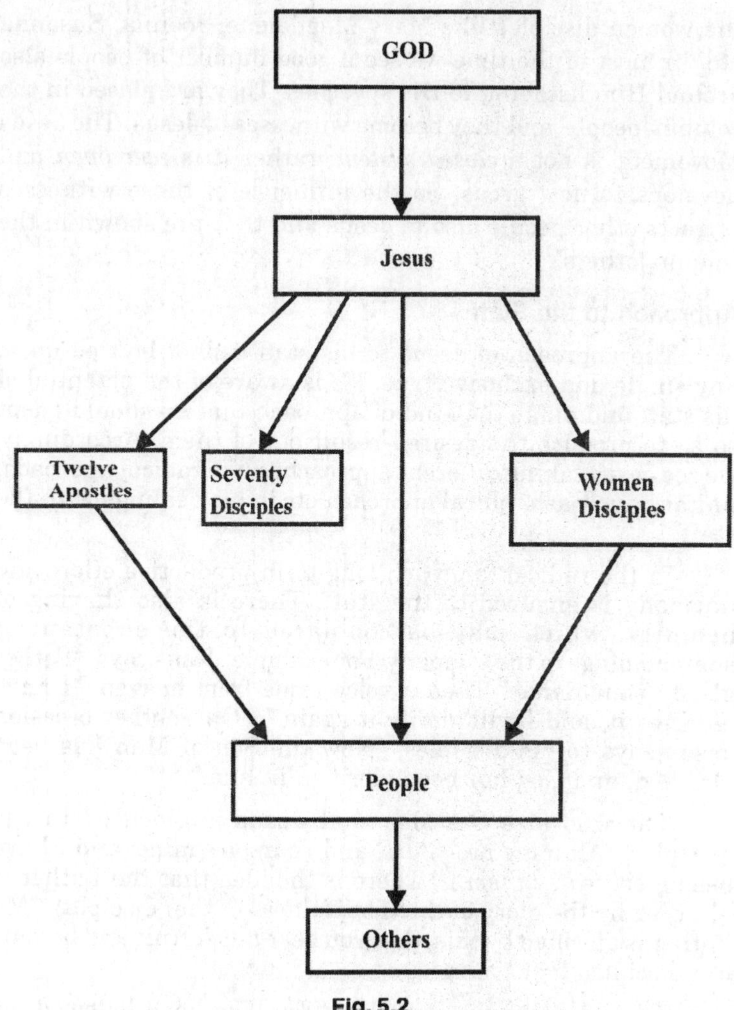

Fig. 5.2

Staff in the Jesus Movement

The above diagram gives a clear-cut idea about the different levels of staff who play different roles in the movement of Jesus. God ɜnds Jesus with a mission or Jesus receives direct ɔwer from God to start His ministry. Jesus proclaims the Kingdom of God to the specially chosen twelve apostles first. At the same time He teaches seventy disciples, the women disciples like Mary Magdalene, Joanna, Susanna etc. In most of the time we see a good number of people also around Him listening to His speeches. They are placed in the column 'people' and they become witnesses to Jesus. The Jesus Movement is not a *closed system*; rather it is *ever open* and develops to new areas. So the influence of those witnesses attracts other people also to Jesus and they are shown in the column 'others'.

Approach to the Staff

The approach of Jesus to his staff cannot be tied up to any single and exclusive type. He is aware of the potential of his staff and plans the kind of approach that he should adopt so as to produce the desired result out of them. Accordingly, we see Jesus taking different approaches like radical approach, unitary approach, plural approach etc in his dealings with the staff.

In the radical approach long-term productive effort and harmony is ensured to the staff. There is also sharing of benefits, which may be compared to the substantial shareholdings in the company. For example, Jesus says, "Father glorify your name." Then a voice came from heaven, "I have glorified it, and I will glorify it again."[52] On another occasion Jesus says to his disciples, "Now the Son of Man has been glorified, and God has been glorified in him."[53]

There is also the idea that Jesus is glorified in the disciples. "All mine are yours, and yours are mine; and I have been *glorified in them.*"[54] There is the idea that the Father is glorified by the glory of the (fruitfulness of the) disciples. "My Father is glorified by this, that you bear much fruit and become my disciples."[55]

Jesus says to the disciples, "You who have followed me will also sit on twelve thrones, judging the twelve tribes of Israel."[56]

Therefore, it seems that Jesus' approach in a sense was similar to the radical approach to the staff. At the same time it is different from it. It is not sharing the Father's glory with the Son or the disciples; rather there is identification of the glory of the Father with the glory of the Son and the glory of the disciples. It is radical, but radical in a spiritual sense. In the spiritual world there is no sharing, but only communion or identification. Sharing is a concept that has relevance only in the material world. Money can be shared, i.e., divided between different claimants. But glory cannot be divided. It is a spiritual concept. That is why the glory of the Father is identified with the glory of the Son and of the disciples.

There are also certain elements of the unitary approach in the approach to the staff of Jesus' Movement. He takes all the necessary steps to harmonise and integrate the disciples' aims, hopes, aspirations and ambitions for the realisation of his main mission of bringing the Kingdom of God. So he transfers his power and authority to each one of them. He kept teaching, sharing and demonstrating his work to his team members. He likes to see them learning and doing the same and greater things in the world. So he promises them, "the one who believes in me will also do the same work that I do, and, in fact, will do greater works than these. ..."[57] He also says to his disciples, "I have made known to you everything that I have heard from my Father."[58] He treats the disciples as equals and tells them, "You are my friends."[59] He gives the right to use his name to do what must be done. "If in my name you ask me for anything, I will do it."[60] Though he had given warning about his death he understands the real shock that will bring to them when it actually happens. So he prepares them saying, "I will not leave you orphaned; I am coming to you."[61] In the second phase of proclaiming Jesus, he guarantees his presence and also the success in their mission. He says to the disciples, "I am with you always, to the end of the age."[62]

All the above-mentioned events give an understanding of Jesus' real interest in bringing up the disciples to his expectations. He is very keen in each step of their development and sincerely desired their growth in the overall perspective.

In the Jesus' Movement we can recognise also certain elements of the plural approach. Plural approach is the recognition of the divergent and often conflicting aims and objectives of the staff and satisfying them. To the disciples who followed Jesus after leaving everything Jesus gives the promise:

> Truly I tell you , there is no one who has left house or brothers or sisters or mother or father or children or fields, for my sake or for the sake of the good news, who will not receive a hundredfold now in this age – houses, brothers and sisters, mothers and children, and fields ..."[63]

The disciples have left different types of their possessions and relationships. Jesus is promising a corresponding reward. That area, which remains unfulfilled because of the discipleship, will be fulfilled by the reward Jesus promises. The person who feels the loss of the mother will be rewarded with the satisfaction of having a mother. Those persons who feel the loss of children will be given the satisfaction of having children. Therefore, there is a correspondence between the need of the disciples and the reward promised. This is what happens for the plural approach of staff. At the same time this approach transcends the plural approach. First of all Jesus does not promise the satisfaction of having a father to those who have left father to follow Jesus. The reason seems to be there is God as the only father for the disciples. This father cannot be substituted by any other experience. Secondly, we know from human experience that the relationship of a family has uniqueness, which cannot be substituted with other relationship. For example, no one can be in the place of one's mother. Therefore, what Jesus means is that there will be reward both in this world and in eternal life and this reward is to be understood as satisfaction from spiritual life.

All the above analysis of texts shows that in the Jesus' Movement there is correspondence and non-correspondence with the Seven-S approach. Specifically speaking about the staff this correspondence and non-correspondence are equally detectable.

Shared Values

In the Jesus' Movement we can also see the shared values as in any organisation. But what are these values? These are values which everyone in the movement recognises, upholds, lives for and makes his or her aim to establish. In a previous section we showed that the strategy of the Jesus' Movement was the establishment of the Kingdom of God. The values are those, which directly or indirectly help the strategy. Therefore, the values of the Jesus' Movement are those values, which help the establishment of the Kingdom of God. These values can be identified as the recognition of God as the supreme authority in one's life and the readiness to forego and subordinate each other value to this supreme value, which is God. Every individual member of the Jesus' Movement and all the staff placed in different levels of responsibility are all to recognise and realise this value. This value is expressed in the Old Testament, as "You shall love the LORD your God with all your heart, and with all your soul, and with all your might."[64] and is appropriated and repeated by Jesus in the New Testament.[65] Parallel to this value is the value of the love of fellow-beings. This is a total and unreserved love. This is expressed in the Old Testament, as "You shall love your neighbour as yourself."[66] and is continued and is directly associated with the love of God in the New Testament.[67] The newness of the love command in the New Testament is in the direct association of the love of neighbour with the love of God. Though these two commandments were there in the Old Testament they were not given equal status or direct relationship. But in the New Testament these two are put together as one value. In other words loving God with one's whole heart, soul and might is practically realised in loving the neighbour as oneself.

In the New Testament we can see also another attempt at clarifying the newness of the commandment. This is in the gospel of John. There the standard to be followed in loving the neighbour is not one's love for oneself, but the standard set by Jesus. Jesus says, "Love one another as I have loved you."[68] This standard of Jesus' love is explained in another part of the gospel. The type of love, which Jesus showed is the love, which makes him, lay down his life for the sheep.[69] This love is further expressed as "No one has greater love than this, to lay down one's life for one's friends."[70]

Thus it becomes clear that the shared value of the Jesus' Movement is love of God expressed in love of neighbour. The standard of this love is the supreme love of Jesus to his friends or disciples. This is the value, which everyone of the Jesus' Movement has to uphold and show in practice.

Skills

As in the Seven-S approach we can recognise the role of skills in the Jesus' Movement. Skills are the abilities that an employee needs for carrying out the strategy of the organisation. From this idea of skills we can identify the skills that were needed in the Jesus' Movement. Among the disciples of Jesus there were people with different responsibilities. Peter was always the head of the disciples. He was the one who functioned as the spokesman of the group. According to Mathew 16:19 he was given the keys of the Kingdom of heaven. Then there is the common status of the twelve apostles. After them there were the seventy disciples. There were also the women disciples. What was the basis on which Jesus appointed these people in different levels of responsibilities? Did he not consider the personal abilities of these people? Probably Peter had certain leadership qualities more than the other disciples. The same way those in other levels of responsibilities also had their personal skills in that field. But we don't have any New Testament evidence to show that these people had different personal abilities or skills. But the fundamental skill required for all the jobs in the Movement seems to be the power to love. As we read in the gospel of John, Peter's leadership position was given on the basis of his ability to love Jesus more than the others. Jesus asks him three times, "Simon, son of John, do you love me more than these?"[71] It is after procuring an unequivocal affirmation from Peter that Jesus appoints him as the leader. Therefore, the one skill that is required of the disciples of Jesus is the skill to love. Depending on the grade in which one acquires this skill he or she is appointed in different levels of responsibilities. Other skills also may be regarded. But we have no definite proof in the New Testament. Whatever may be the value of other skills they are all subordinate to this one skill, the skill to love.

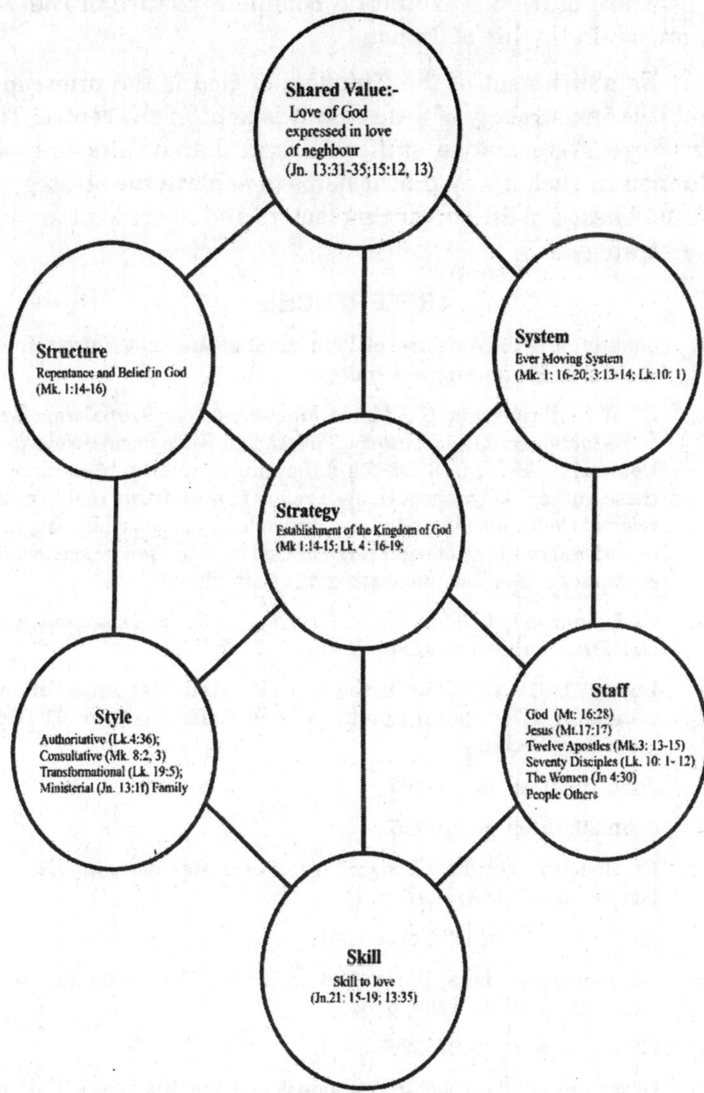

Fig. 5.3

7-S Approach in the Jesus' Movement

The Figure 5.3 exhibits a complete picture of the 7-S approach in the life of Jesus.

Establishment of the Kingdom of God is the prime aim and it is the strategy of Jesus. So it is kept in the centre. The structure, system, style, staff, skill, and shared value are well planned in such a way that it helps to achieve the strategy of Jesus. These are the supporting factors and so are kept around the strategy.

REFERENCES

1. Johannine is the Adjective of John and it means that which belongs to John or Pertaining to John.

2. Cf. W.F Albright and G.S Mann, *Mathew, A New Translation With Introduction and Commentary*, The Anchor Bible Series, New York, Doubleday, 1971, p. 6 for the difference in nuance. According to these authors kingdom of Heaven refers to the earthly reality of the reign of God, which is guided and controlled by Jesus while Kingdom of God refers to the eternal reign of God over human beings, which continues even after the death of the individuals.

3. Cf. Leonardo Boff, *Jesus Christ Liberator: A Critical Christology for Our Time*, Orbis Books, New York, 1997, pp. 52-55.

4. Luke 4:18-19 as given in the New Revised Standard Version, Bangalore, Theological Publications in India, 2003, p. 61 (New Testament Section).

5. John 10:10, op. cit., p. 103.

6. John 20:31, op. cit., p. 115.

7. Cf. Joachim Gnilka, *Jesus of Nazareth: Message and History*, Hendrickson, USA, 1997, p. 81.

8. Mark. 1:14-16, op. cit., p. 35.

9. Cf. John Desrochers, *Christ The Liberator*, The Centre for Social Action, Bangalore, 1997, p. 64.

10. Cf. Isaiah 40:9; 41:27; 52:7; 61: 1.

11. In the present day scholarly opinion is that the first book of the New Testament is the first letter to the Thessalonians which is Believed to be Written About 48 A.D.

12. Cf. Leonardo Boff, *Jesus Christ Liberator: A Critical Christology for Our Time*, Orbis Books, New York, 1997, pp. 286-287.

13. Mark 1:15, op. cit., p. 35.

14. Mark. 1:16-20, op. cit., p. 35.
15. Mark. 3:13-14, op. cit., p. 37.
16. Cf. Luke 8:1-3 op. cit., p. 67.
17. Mark 2:12, op. cit., p. 36.
18. Mark 1:27, op. cit., p. 35.
19. Cf. Mark 1:25, op. cit., p. 35.
20. Cf. Mark 1:31, op. cit., p. 35.
21. Mark 1:41, op. cit., p. 35.
22. Cf. Mark 1:16-20; 2:14, op. cit., pp. 35, 36.
23. Mathew 23:37-39, op. cit., p. 26.
24. Mark 8:1-2, op. cit., p. 43.
25. Luke 19:8.
26. Cf. John 4:5-41.
27. Mathew 20:25-27, op. cit., p. 22.
28. Mathew 20:25-27, op. cit., p. 22. The Son of Man is the English literal translation of the Aramaic Phrase *Barnasa*. Literally it means Son of Man and in its use it means Any Man. This phrase is used in a technical sense in the New Testament always to refer to Jesus that too in his own words. In short Son of Man means "I" the first person singular in the words of Jesus.
29. Mt.16:28, op. cit., p. 18.
30. Cf. Mt. 16:13-19, op. cit., p. 18.
31. Mt. 17: 17, op. cit., p. 19.
32. Mt. 23: 38-39, op. cit., p. 26.
33. Mark 3: 13-15, op. cit., p. 37.
34. Mark 3:20-21, op. cit., p. 37.
35. Cf. Mark 4:10, op. cit., p. 38.
36. The Samaritans are a half Jewish tribe having almost the same faith as the Jews. But due to historical reasons they were separated by the other Jews and were considered as low in status than the Jews. (Cf. J.L. McKenzie, Dictionary of the Bible, London, Geoffrey Chapman, 1965) Gentiles "is a Generic Term used for People other than Jews and Samaritans.
37. Mt. 28:18-20, op. cit., p. 34.

38. Mk. 6:12-13, op. cit., p. 40.
39. Cf. Mt. 17:16, op. cit., p. 19.
40. Cf. Luke 10:1-12.
41. Luke 10:1.
42. Cf. Luke 24: 18, op. cit., p. 90.
43. Compare Acts 1: 14 with Acts 2: 1, p. 118, 119.
44. N.K. Gottwald and R.A. Horsley, *The Bible and Liberation: Political and Social Hermeneutics*, op. cit., p. 457.
45. Cf. Luke 8: 1-3, op. cit., p. 67.
46. Cf. N.K. Gottwald and R.A. Horsley, The Bible and Liberation: Political and Social Hermeneutics, op. cit., p. 457.
47. Cf. Acts 2: 1, op. cit., p. 119.
48. John 4: 29, op. cit., p. 95.
49. John 4: 30, op. cit., p. 95.
50. John 20: 17, op. cit., p. 115.
51. Cf. John 20: 18, op. cit., p. 115.
52. John 12: 28, op. cit., p. 106.
53. John 13: 31, op. cit., p. 108.
54. John 17: 10, op. cit., p. 111.
55. John 15: 8, op. cit., p. 109.
56. Mathew 19: 28, op. cit., p. 21.
57. John 14: 12, op. cit., p. 109.
58. John 15: 15, op. cit., p. 109.
59. John 15: 14, op. cit., p.109.
60. John 14: 14, op. cit., p. 109.
61. John 14: 18, op. cit., p. 109.
62. Mathew 28: 20, op. cit., p. 34.
63. Mark 10: 29-30, op. cit., p. 46.
64. Deuteronomy 6: 5, op. cit., p. 163 (Old Testament Section).
65. Mathew 22:37, p. 25; Mark 12:30, p. 49; Luke 10:27, p. 71.
66. Levi. 19:18, op. cit., p. 106 (Old Testament Section).

67. Mt. 19:19, p. 21; 22:39 p. 25; Mk. 12:31, 12:33 p. 49.

68. John 15:12, op. cit., p. 109.

69. Cf. John. 10:15, op. cit., p. 103.

70. John. 15:13, op. cit., p. 109.

71. John 21:15, 16, 17.

6

Beyond Seven–S

As already pointed out the 7-S approach is a great advancement in the field of management in recent years. The first and foremost merit of this approach is that it does not narrow down management to any single idea or principle. The problem with the other approaches was that they put forward one or other single principle as the basic requirement for successful management. The very fact that each approach had a different basic principle is itself proof that none of them qualifies for the one basic principle by the acquisition of which all problems connected with the management can be solved. There is also a misconception of human behaviour behind these approaches. The people who have put forward these approaches seem to think that there is one basic principle, which explains the total human behaviour. For some, the correct approach for the management is the case approach or the empirical approach, i.e., learning to do things by doing. It seems to presuppose that we cannot approach management with any training in the field because only by doing things in concrete situations and solving problems in those situations the manager can acquire training for management. The approaches like inter-personal behaviour approach, group behaviour approach, co-operative social system approach and so on narrow down management to one or other principle. On the other hand the 7-S approach presupposes the complexity of the human behaviour and therefore seven principles are proposed. When we praise the 7-S approach we do affirm that the human behaviour is certainly a complex reality. Our idea may be summarised as follows: There can be or cannot be one single principle behind all human behaviour. Even if there is one single principle we have not identified that one principle and we are not sure that even in the future we will be able to identify that one principle. At present all that we learn about human behaviour is that it is a complex reality because it appears in diverse forms. Therefore in our present condition it is always advisable that we approach management with the presupposition that human behaviour is a complex reality. In this regard the 7-S approach is more commendable because it speaks of seven approaches and not one single approach.

The Limitations

Though there are such positive qualities in the 7-S approach we have to ask certain questions to the 7-S approach itself.

The Naming

First of all the very name 'Seven-S' seems to be artificial. This name is made possible by starting the names of all the seven approaches with the letter 'S'. This naming is artificial. For example the approach called 'shared value' could better be called common value system because it is about having a common value which everyone connected with the organisation or firm believes and approves. But in the 7-S approach it is artificially called 'shared value' just to give it a name starting with the letter 'S'.

The Numbering

Another problem with this approach is the problem of the number 'seven'. Are we able to say that there are seven approaches and only seven approaches to management? Can there not be an eighth or ninth approach? How can we definitely say that there are only seven approaches to management? Is not there the influence of the Western tradition, which sees the number seven as the perfect number? But this belief is really superstitious. There is also the problem whether those who propose the 7-S approach have exhausted all the possible approaches to the management. It seems that they have proposed the seven approaches because seven were the problems they had to tackle. But we cannot deny that there can be an eighth or ninth problem, which also needs a particular approach for solution.

Is Shared Value Possible?

Another problem with this approach is concerning the cultural difference of the people. All that is applicable in a Western context need not apply in the same way in the Eastern hemisphere. What is a value for the Westerner may not be a value for the Easterner. Also something held to be a value today need not continue as a value tomorrow. In ethics there is a vast area, which is governed by situation, and the people involved. Therefore, shared value becomes almost impossible. If the manager is a European with progressive idea and the employees are people from undeveloped Eastern villages how can there be shared values held by the manager and the employees?

Charismatic Quality

The opinions expressed by some recent management thinkers and the suggestions proposed by them also point to the insufficiency of the 7-S approach. We will look into some of these recent opinions and suggestions. In 1998 Herb Greenberg came out showing the importance of charismatic leadership in management. Greenberg does not define it. Without defining he tries to describe the qualities of such people. According to him, "charismatic leaders are those rare individuals who can chart a course, fill people with a new sense of purpose, light a fire that encourages people to reach further than they've reached before, and somehow make the distance between the starting point and the goal seem shorter than it really is."[1] About the usefulness of charisma he says that it is, "an elusive quality that's hard to put your finger on, but it somehow makes us all feel privileged to be around such people. Where others see problems, leaders see opportunities."[2] This suggestion seems to propose that charismatic quality is something desirable in management. But the 7-S approach does not have such an approach. It seems to be something beyond the proposed 7-S approach to management.

Learning and Applying Skills

Tim Hannagan has a different approach. He says, "Successful managers are those who have learned the appropriate body of knowledge and have developed an ability to apply acquired skills and techniques."[3] Here he distinguishes between the acquired skills and techniques on the one hand and the ability to apply them on the other. It seems that according to him it is not enough to acquire skills and techniques. They can be acquired through learning. Over and above such skills and techniques there is the need for the ability to apply them. Where do we get this ability? Is it something that can be learned from books or classes? In his own words, "successful managers are those *born* with appropriate *intuition*, intelligence and personality which they develop through the practice of leadership. Leadership skill can be developed although not taught."[4] This suggestion needs a little elaboration. According to this author there is an aspect of management, which a person receives by birth and it cannot be taught. But what is gained by birth can be developed. In other words there is an inborn aspect of management. This also is something beyond the 7-S approach.

Affiliative Interest

This same author, i.e., Tim Hannagan, speaks of another aspect of management, which he calls *affiliative interest*. What he means by affiliative interest is "a care and concern for the feelings of others, but not at the expense of getting the job done. It is a concern for the legitimate needs and feelings of others, which is the type of affiliation that will lead to greater organisational effectiveness."[5] To which of the seven approaches shall we connect affiliative interest? It seems that it stands outside of the 7-S approach. In other words it also is a quality beyond the 7-S. The same quality seems to be hinted at by another writer by name Sumantra Ghoshal. In an article he says, "except for a pathological few, most people have an innate preference for helping others."[6] This 'innate preference for helping others seems to be the same as Hannagan's 'affiliative interest'. Anyway this is not something listed in the 7-S approach.

Spirituality and Management

According to a report that came in the Malayalam daily 'Mathrubhoomi' there is an increased interest in spirituality among the government employees in Kerala.[7] The same thing is reported by Jon Watkins in the previous year. He says that "in the nineties spirituality attempts to encompass business ethics, environmental concern, socio-economic values and a rejection of hard-nosed capitalism."[8] Jon Watkins quotes Richard Cree who says, "I think the evidence is there to suggest that the interest in spirituality among employees is certainly increasing. You can tell that just by increase in the amount of research, such as that done by Roffey Park."[9] These suggestions show that there is a place for spirituality also in management. This also is something that lies beyond 7-S.

The new interest in spirituality is to be properly analysed and examined. Sometimes this interest can be an escape from responsibility. In other words a person who is tired of his responsibilities within the firm may seek a break from these responsibilities by adhering to spiritual practices. Sometimes this can distract him from his responsibility and slowly lessen the interest in the firm and bring to a situation of complete break away from his responsibilities. This means we have to be cautious about evaluating the interest in spirituality.

On the other hand this interest is also a pointer to an inherent need in the human personality. That means, a person's life cannot be confined to his work in an organisation or a firm. There are aspects of human personality, which are not fulfilled by his involvement and dedication to the firm. Therefore, to keep a person healthy in his integral personality appropriate importance should be given to satisfy his spiritual need. This satisfaction will keep the person integral and whole and keep him healthy and when a person is fully healthy, physically and mentally he can apply himself better to his responsibility.

Ethics

Another area which needs closer examination and which is closely related to spirituality is ethics. What is the importance of ethics in management? This question can be answered only if we realise the importance of ethics in human life. What distinguishes a human person from the animal world is that he has a sense of right and wrong in his action. Anything human beings do contains in it this aspect, which is not found in the actions of the animals and the birds. Anything man does is either right or wrong. This right-ness and wrong-ness is not decided by the success or failure of the action in relation to the goal of management. Even an action not related to the factory or firm where one works has an aspect of right-ness and wrong-ness. Therefore, management cannot exist without giving due thought to the ethical aspect of human actions. If an action is at variance with ethical principles that will affect the peace of mind of the doer and that will have its effect on his or her performance.

> If the manager...were to make peace with himself or herself and set his/her mind at being one with the environment would peace not prevail? And what can be a better catalyst for growth than peace of mind? ... It means simply that through ethical conduct the manager must realise a level of consciousness, which allows him to be objective, and detached while making value based decisions.[10]

In this connection it is important to give attention to a complaint voiced by Easo John. He says that a Christian believer finds himself in conflict with accepted principles of ethics when he yields to the designs of the firm where he is working. He says,

> There are many Christians in various responsible positions who are bewildered as I was. They see limited options that are available and all of them are apparently in conflict with what they believe it to be right.[11]

The same opinion is voiced by J.A. Petrick and J.F. Quinn. They say that Ethics and managerial performance and integrity are proportionate to each other. A balanced position on ethics will increase the performance of the person involved.[12]

Ethics as such does not come under the 7-S approach. It is true that the 7-S approach speaks about shared value. But how shared values are related to ethics is not clear. First of all shared value is to be seen within the confinement of the successful performance of the firm or the organisation. A value concerning the running of the firm and its success is to be common for the manager and the employees. But ethics which is concerned about human actions is measured not with any material gain. It is about the action in itself unrelated to material gain or loss. Therefore, ethics also is to be understood as something that lies beyond the 7-S.

The Recognition of the Divine in the Human

According to the above analysis, the aspects of managerial approach that lie beyond the 7-S are charismatic quality, learning and applying skill, affiliative interest, spirituality and ethics. But are they the only qualities, which lie beyond the 7-S approach? Need not be. An intuitive mind may be able to identify many more aspects of management approach, which lie beyond the 7-S approach. But a total listing and identification of them is not important from our point of view. It is not the number and the identity, which is important for us. Rather the fact that there are such aspects and the source of such aspects are important for our consideration. What is that which underlies these aspects of management, which lie beyond the 7-S approach? It seems quite clear that all those qualities, which we have identified, have a common characteristic. They are of a divine nature. For example, the affiliative interest is not directly related to the material success of the organisation. In fact, caring for the individual needs of the employees will only result in immediate loss to the firm though there will be gain in the longer run. So it is like opting for failure for the sake of success as Mahesh Murthy says, "It does not matter whether you're a winner or not in the world's eyes. But it does matter that you stood up for what you believe in."[13] In this connection it is interesting to note that some people who have climbed the ladder of success are too childish in their human personality and such a success cannot be a desirable success. As Rhymer Rigby puts it:

> You must remember that most people who get to the top of businesses give up almost everything to get there. They're pretty well one stick short of a bundle, psychologically unbalanced even. I would say what they need to get there means that in other areas of their lives they're probably 18 years old or less—and they're 80 years old in terms of business.[14]

All the above comments point to a factor, which needs development and elucidation in order to have an integral growth of the personality and a balanced development of business. This aspect we name as a divine aspect.

When we say this is a divine aspect we mean that it is an aspect, which is related to an element in man, which is not fully explained by a material and empirical analysis of human behaviour and capabilities. We can explain it with the examples of certain individuals in history who have been wonderfully successful in their areas of activities without at the same time any extra-ordinary training or other equipment.

Mother Teresa

Mother Teresa has the largest number of followers in the Catholic Church. She has convents in all the continents of the world. At the time of her death, Mother Teresa's Missionaries of Charity had more than 4,000 sisters, an associated brotherhood of 300 members, and more than 1,00,000 lay volunteers, operating 610 missions in 123 countries.[15] These included hospices and homes for people with HIV/AIDS, leprosy and tuberculosis, soup kitchens, children's and family counselling programmes, orphanages, and schools. All these she achieved in the second half of her life. That is after her call to be the Redeemer of the Poor. She not only attracted so many people to join her congregation, she was also able to keep them united through her charismatic personality. What made her have such a success in her life when there are untold difficulties in keeping peace among the members of other congregations with much less number of members? The number of charitable institutions, which Mother Teresa started in her lifetime, is much more than what other congregations were able to do in a time of centuries. And more than all these the history of India tells us that no woman of India has received such an honorable funeral like Mother Teresa. No politician, social worker or religious leader has received such honour or respect in his or her funeral. Just by counting the number of people who have attended her funeral one can say that she was the greatest woman leader of modern India. Nay, the greatest and most loved woman leader of the world at large. Her death was widely considered a great loss within both secular and religious communities. The former U.N. Secretary-General Javier Perez de Cuellar, for example, said: "She is the United Nations. She is peace in the world." Nawaz Sharif, the Prime Minister of Pakistan said that Teresa was "A rare and unique individual who lived long for higher purposes. Her life-long devotion to the care of the poor, the sick, and the disadvantaged was one of the highest examples of service to humanity." What is the secret that worked behind her leadership? From all considerations she was just an ordinary woman. She had no formal training in management studies. She had no qualities and achievements in political field. Her achievement in the literary field is almost nil and her authority in the religious society to which she belongs also is negligible. Yet she has attracted more people to her funeral than any poet or artist or politician or religious leader of India was able to draw in his or her funeral. If her success is not measurable by empirical methods then the only conclusion that is possible is that she had recourse to some power that lies beyond the reach of empirical measurement. Let us call it the divine. In other words Mother Teresa had contact with this divine element, which is invisibly active in the human spheres of activities. And how did she come in contact with this power? It is, as we can express in our human language, is with faith and a life in accordance with that faith.

John Paul II

The beginning of Pope John Paul II is very humble and ordinary. As we read from his life history, by the time he became a young man he had become almost an orphan with no parents or close relatives. Poverty had brought him to stone quarries to work there as a daily worker to earn his livelihood, and to other factories. He had formal education in theology. But that was just enough for ordination as a priest. He had literary talents. But in comparison to the output of the great literary men in the world his talents were most negligible. In spite of all these lack of training and talents he rose in fame and leadership and came to the topmost position in the Catholic Church. That is he became the Pope. But Popes there have been many. What distinguishes John Paul II as a great man is not his position as the Pope of the Church. Why So many – almost two hundred political leaders from all over the world attended his funeral and why around four million people thronged to Rome to be present at the funeral service and why innumerable people all over the world witnessed the last rites of this man on the televisions? Are we able to answer these questions by recourse to any tangible and empirical aspect of his life? If not, we are inevitably forced to say that he had contact with something that lies beyond the reach of human measurement and received help from it, for the successful performance as a leader. Let us call it his faith in the divine.

The Beyond in the Biblical Management

In the previous chapters we analysed the managerial performance of two leaders of the Bible and brought to light how they have applied the 7-S approach in their lives. We chose one leader each from the Old Testament and the New Testament, Moses and Jesus respectively. Already in our analysis of their particular way of doing things we have come across both identity and difference. They have applied, as we have shown the 7-S approach in their method and yet they had their own different way to this approach. Now let us take the lives of these two Biblical leaders and see how they were receiving help from an invisible power, the divine power with which they had contact through faith.

The Beyond in Moses' Management

The strategy of the Liberation Movement led by Moses was identified as making the people, the People of God, a people dedicated to God. This strategy is different from other strategies used by firms and organisations in its basic quality. In ordinary organisations a strategy consists of doing certain things or achieving certain things especially achieving revolutionary growth in production or very high quality of the products.[16] In short strategy consists in achievement. But in the case of Moses' Movement of Liberation no such goal is set as the strategy of the Movement. It is becoming the People of God. In other words while in other organisations achieving is the strategy, in Moses' Movement becoming is the strategy.

In the system used in Moses' Liberation Movement we have God, a revealing God at the top of the system. While speaking about the style of Moses we pointed to the fact that it was a complex style. In the staff we identified God as standing at the topmost position. The shared value was liberty under God and as to the skill, the basic skill applied in Moses' Movement we identified as the fear of God. All these are fundamentally different from the approaches used in ordinary business. Basic to all these is the skill applied by Moses. As we have identified it is the fear of God, which was the one skill that Moses applied all through the Liberation Movement. There is need for further elaboration of this skill.

What we know about the early history of Moses is that he was brought up in Egypt under the care and protection of the daughter of the king. He had no contact with the people whom he was to liberate in the future. As we read in the Book of Exodus only after growing up into a young man he sees his people for the first time.[17] In the palace of Pharaoh, the Egyptian king, he had no training about leading the slaves out of the house of slavery. But when he received the commission to be the liberator he does it very beautifully and successfully in spite of the fact that the people were very rough and uncouth. All that they knew about their tradition was that they were the sons of Abraham, Isaac, and Jacob. God himself was introduced to them as the God of their fathers, Abraham, Isaac, and Jacob. They had no other training in any human qualities. They also had no will power to resist the king and his taskmasters who were keeping them as slaves. When Moses was asked to bring this people out of slavery he was dealing with an unknown people. Yet he was successful. What was the power that was at work in Moses and what was the source of that power? As we can learn from the pages of the Bible the only power at work in Moses was the firm faith he had in God.[18] This led him through times of tensions and difficulties and enlightened his heart when he was unsure of the path he should take and this power he shared to the people and brought them out of slavery.

The Beyond in Jesus' Management

In one of the previous chapters where we dealt with managerial practice of Jesus we spoke about the 7-S approach used by Jesus. In connection with the style adopted by Jesus, we said that the best name for the Jesus' style of functioning would be 'family style'. In the same way about the shared value we said love of God expressed in love of neighbour is the value that is shared by all who are involved in the Jesus Movement. About the skill we said that the particular skill that is applied in Jesus' Movement is above everything else, the skill to love. All these point to the speciality of the managerial functioning of Jesus. About the staff we said God is placed at the topmost position in the ladder of responsible persons. Why Jesus succeeded in his movement is because he received power, a hidden power for that matter from his special relationship with God.[19]

Now the question of success is very much debatable. One may ask did Jesus succeed, a person mercilessly killed on the cross? Jesus' success cannot be measured by the criteria we use for other organisations and business establishments. First of all success does not consist in the popular opinion about it. Success is not measured by the quality and quantity of the goal achieved by an organisation. Jesus' strategy was the establishment of the kingdom of God and this aim he achieved most successfully in his own life and in the life of those who were related to him. In that sense Jesus' Movement was a total success. In this connection it is in place to quote an opinion expressed by V.P. Michael about the successful managerial functioning of Jesus. He says,[20]

> No wonder why an ordinary person, Jesus, who lived in almost obscurity till the age of 30 has been able to influence millions and millions of people to follow him faithfully for the last 2000 years. Many great men have given up themselves to be martyrs for Christ. One of the greatest philosophers of first century A.D., Paul had remarked, "I am not ashamed, for I know whom I have believed, and am persuaded that he is able to keep that which I have committed unto him."[21]

So it is unquestionable. Jesus was a great success. He lived himself the life of the Kingdom of God and attracted many millions down through the centuries to realise the Kingdom of God in their own lives.

The most ordinary man Jesus, the one who qualified himself as having no where to lay his head has left a legacy which is more precious than any product coming out from any factory or firm. What was the power that was working in him? It is not any formal training in any business management or any training at all. But it was the special relationship or faith he had with God, his Father.

> Faith for the Old and New Testaments is the power to say yes and Amen to God as God is discovered through life by existing with and basing oneself on God as the absolute meaning of all things; it is a continuous returning to and grasping on to God. According to this definition, Jesus was an extraordinary believer and had faith. Faith was Jesus' way of life. He always allowed himself to be determined by God and the other.[22]

To conclude, we have examined the functioning of the two leaders of the Bible. Both of them received special strength from their relationship with God. This strength was above anything that was possible to be acquired through formal training. For an ordinary man today the means to have relationship with God is faith. Therefore, we can put forward faith in God as a factor, which should be considered as most important in the field of management.

The two persons we have taken, as example from the Bible had no formal training, but only the special relationship with God as the weapon for their successful functioning. But if this weapon is added to formal training then the person who has it will be able to function more successfully. Our thesis is not that any training is unnecessary. Rather we suggest that training should be supplemented with faith in the Supreme Being. If both these go hand in hand then the manager will be able to face any situation and come out successful in his endeavours. Seven-S approach is a very recent, remarkable and well-experimented approach to management. But it does not consider the spiritual aspect of man, the fact that every human being is a son or daughter of God, his or her creator and Father. A filial relationship with this Father will enhance the skills that are gained through formal training. Only then the manager becomes a fully human being because the manager as a human being is not simply a bundle of flesh and blood or of intellectual faculty but also and primarily a spiritual being, a being who is related to the Supreme Spiritual Being whom we call God. Due consideration to this aspect of man will force the manager to expend himself or herself fully in his or her field of activities. That is the clue to successful management.

REFERENCES

1. H. Greenberg, "Controlling Charisma", *Sales and Marketing Management*, September 1998, p. 22.
2. Ibid.
3. Tim Hannagan, *Management Concepts and Practice*, Delhi, Macmillan India Ltd., 1997, p. 639.
4. Ibid.
5. Tim Hannagan, Management Concepts and Practice, op. cit., p. 342.
6. Sumantra Ghoshal, "Something's Got To Give", *People Management*, February 12, 2004, p. 3.
7. Cf. *Mathrubhoomi*, March 30, 2004, p. 3
8. Jon Watkins, "Spiritual Guidance", *People Management*, February 20, 2003, p. 16.
9. Ibid.

10. S. Sadri and others, *The Theory and Practice of Managerial Ethics*, Mumbai, Jaico Publishing House, 1999, p. 85

11. E. John, *Christian Perspective on Management*, Chennai, Easo John Associates, 2003, p. 2.

12. Cf. J.A. Petrick and J.F. Quinn, *Management Ethics*, New Delhi, Response Books, 1997, pp. 65-66.

13. Mahesh Murthy, "We have to Fail to Succeed", *Business World*, 16th February, 2004, p. 58.

14. R. Rigby, "The Path to Power", *Management Today*, September 1998, p. 46.

15. Cf. M. K. Paul, *Blessed Teresa of Kolkata*, Mumbai, St. Pauls, 2004, p. 23.

16. Cf. The Strategy of the Matushitha Company Explained in *The Art of Japanese Management* by R.T. Pascale and A.G. Athos, New York, Penguin Books, 1981.

17. Cf. Exodus. 2: 11, op. cit., p. 49

18. Cf. G. W. Coats, The Moses Tradition, op. cit., p. 75

19. Cf. Antony Kalliath cmi (editor), *Christian Leadership: The Shifting Focus in Theological Education*, Bangalore, Dharmaram Publications, Dharmaram College, 2001, p. 72.

20. V.P.Michael, *Management for Managers*, Bombay,Himalaya Publishing House,1992, p. 160.

21. 2 Thimothy 1: 12.

22. Leonardo Boff, *Jesus Christ Liberator: A Critical Christology for Our Time*, op. cit., p. 113.

7

General Conclusion

From the long analysis of the evolution of management as an art and a science we have observed that there are different schools of thought on the evolution of Management. The four stages in its evolution, over a period of hundred years covers the scientific approach to management, through contributors and thinkers like Robert Owen, Charles Babbage, F.W. Taylor, H.L. Gantt, Gilbreths, Henry Fayol, Elton Mayo, Mary Parker Follett, C.I. Bernard and the like. Management thought in the human relationship era is also covered. The study also covers the integrated management thought. We understand the merits and limitations of various approaches to management beginning from the 'case approach' to 'management process approach'.

The Seven-S approach of McKenzie has certain positive advantages over other approaches in terms of application and empirical evidences. This approach is built upon the pillars of strategy, structure, system, style, staff, shared value and skill. Through the study of the management approaches of two leaders of the Bible we are now able to arrive at a general conclusion to this research study. Researchers and students of management have proposed various methods, which were later found to be insufficient or inadequate or not fully adequate. The 7-S approach was proposed as an improved and unfailing approach to management. The wide acceptance this approach has received from all over the world and the great advances it could make in the field of management have proved its merits over/against many other approaches. At the same time the very recent management thinkers have proposed new elements to be added for successful performance in the field of management. This means the 7-S approach, in spite of its being a very successful approach, is not fully free from problems and defects. This research study in this field seems to take us to the conclusion that what was lacking in the 7-S approach was that it took into consideration only the physical aspect of the question. Management is a field where humans are involved and humans are complex beings with an aspect that goes beyond the realm of the physical.

The study examines the lives of two great role models whose history is depicted in the Holy Bible. These role models had their own unique leadership styles which had in it the elements of McKenzie's Seven-S strategy. The leadership models covered are Moses from the Old Testament and Jesus from the New Testament.

Moses had a clear mission to achieve for which he formulated his own strategy. All that Moses does is in view of achieving this goal. That forming into a people of God is the ultimate strategy is clear in the mission of Moses. So it is clear that being the Son of God and worshipping God is the act by which the people of God define themselves. Therefore worshipping is not the ultimate aim rather being the people of God is the aim and that is the strategy of Moses. His strategy in liberating the enslaved Jews was internalised and well conceived.

For the realisation of his mission Moses makes use of a definite structure. It consists of:

1. Getting the people out of Egypt.
2. Mediating a covenant between God and the people by means of which these people who were slaves will become a free people in an intimate relationship with God.
3. The preservation of the status as the people of God through a religious and social system.

Moses evolved a system which was in tune with his mission. On the top is the eternal plan of God and at the other end or the lowest end is the people (including Pharaoh) to whom the plan of God is communicated and in between the two extremes is placed Moses with Aaron his assistant. These three factors are very intimately inter-related. God speaks not to the people directly, but to Moses and he is the one who communicates God's plan to the people. Yet we have to keep in mind a very important distinction between this system and the ordinary systems in our organisations and firms.

Moses' style is a very complex style. It had different elements in it. Predominantly it was paternalistic. But he also made use of other styles to support and maintain the paternalistic style. The leadership styles adopted by Moses while leading the people from Egypt to Canaan were authoritative, consultative, expert, and paternal. Though these were the different styles he adopted in accordance with the situations, an in-depth study reveals that among these styles paternal was his common style.

What is the staff or the human resource that is applied in the liberation movement led by Moses? If we take all persons and powers involved in the movement we can identify four levels in the organisational structure conceived by Moses—God at the topmost, Moses in close communion with God, Aaron who is Moses' assistant and spokesman, and the tribal leaders through whom Moses gives directives to the people and who accompany him on certain occasion to meet God on Mount Sinai. Thus Moses positions himself ideally and gets things done through right men under him.

Shared value is the value that inspires all the people involved in an organisation, the value shared by the manager, the employees, the sales personnel etc. Now the question in the Liberation Movement of Moses is "what was the central value?" It seems liberty under God was the value shared by Moses, the people and all others involved in the Movement. Everybody wanted to be free and get out of the situation of slavery and this is the shared value of the Liberation Movement of Moses.

Skills are used in a particular situation either to solve a crisis or to boost a particular activity. With this basic idea of skill if we look at the Liberation Movement of Moses we can say that the fear of God is the skill applied throughout the movement. That is the ability with which all people involved in the movement tackle the situation. It is just the fear of God, which made Moses to take up the mission entrusted to him in spite of the fact that he was not an eloquent speaker. It is this fear of the LORD, which made the people honour him and also fear him and made them obey his commands. Fear of the LORD is a concept that needs some explanation. It is not fear in the ordinary sense of the word. It is a technical expression in the Bible and it includes devotion to God and close relationship with Him and a changed personality in consequence to the devotion and close relationship.

The leadership styles and managerial approaches of Jesus Christ is examined considering his dual personality viz. his physical existence as man and his spiritual existence as God. The very birth of Jesus Christ was as per the will of God and with a mission. This mission was to liberate mankind from sin and bring them in harmony with God.

As an ordinary human being, there are numerous instances in the life of Jesus where he pursues a managerial approach which follows the 7-S sequence.

Jesus had a mission which was, 'the establishment of the Kingdom of God'. The strategy adopted was to convey the superiority of spiritualism over materialism and the dominance of eternal life. Creating a strong urge for eternity and salvation through the grace of God is seen throughout in his teachings and fellowships.

The mission of Jesus was to be carried forth through a two fold spiritual structural framework. They are *repentance* or *metanoia* and the experience of a new situation in life, a situation of liberation from all sorts of bindings and captivities and the experience of freedom. Jesus' Movement took a system shape over a period of time. In the first place we have only Jesus, single-handed, proclaiming the good news. Slowly certain disciples are called who were meant for being sent by him to proclaim the good news. Then there are certain others who were also being trained by Jesus. But about this group and their training we have no reference in the gospel. This people also assist Jesus as preachers. Then there are a group of women who provide for Jesus and the disciples. It is a mobile system as we read from Luke 8: 1, moving from town to town and from village to village. It was not founded on a particular place or an office. But it has some sort of an inter-dependant existence and in that sense it was being shaped into a system. What name shall we give it? Let us call it a '**mobile system**' or '**ever moving system**' that aspires for eternal life.

We have seen many aspects of the style of functioning of Jesus. There is authority, compassion, consultation, servant like attitude, severe criticism, fatherly concern etc. That means Jesus' style is a mixed style and no single name can be assigned. Yet the fatherly concern is the dominant attitude. Even when he criticises the Jewish officials it is out of compassion for them and sorrow at their inability to be converted. Therefore it is a many faceted style. What name shall we use for it? Let us call it a 'family style' because in the family the father has compassion, he shows authority, comes down on children with criticism, but never puts them down. Father always, the ideal father at least desires the good of the family members. Therefore, let us qualify the style of Jesus as the '**family style**'.

We have different category of persons in the staff of Jesus' Movement. God the Father is on the topmost position. It is His Kingdom that Jesus came to establish. Next in the ladder is Jesus who is irreplaceable announcer and bringer of the Kingdom. Then we have the twelve apostles who share all the authorities of Jesus including the authority to cast out demons. In the next step are the seventy. They have all authorities except the one to cast out demons. After them stand the women who provide for Jesus and the disciples, who share in proclaiming Jesus in his earthly life and also after his resurrection.

It becomes clear that the shared value of Jesus' Movement is *love of God expressed in love of neighbour*. The standard of this love is the supreme love of Jesus to his friends or disciples. This is the value, which everyone of Jesus' Movement has to uphold and show in practice.

The one skill that is required of the disciples of Jesus is the skill to love. Depending on the grade in which one acquires this skill he or she is appointed in different levels of responsibilities. Other skills also may be regarded. But we have no definite proof in the New Testament. Whatever may be the value of other skills they are all subordinate to this one skill, the skill to love.

There is a spiritual aspect in man which functions as the centre from which every other function in man is controlled and guided. If this spiritual realm is properly taken care of then there is more possibility for success in the field of management. The spirit in man can be properly guided and oriented by his contact with the Absolute Spiritual Being, whom we call God. Faith and life in accordance with faith are the means for contact with this Absolute Being, as all the religions propose. This conclusion is confirmed by the lives and mode of activity of the two examples of managers we took from the pages of the Bible namely Moses and Jesus. We can identify all the items of 7-S approach in their lives. But they were guided and directed by something beyond this 7-S. This something that lies beyond 7-S in their lives is the power they received from their contact with the Absolute Being. In other words behind the success of Moses and Jesus there is something beyond the 7-S approach. This conclusion is further confirmed from history.

Two great leaders from recent history are taken as models to confirm our findings, a woman and a man. They are Mother Teresa of India and John Paul II of Vatican. The extraordinary success of these two individuals in influencing the different realms of social existence and the huge crowd of friends and admirers they could attract speak in unequivocal terms that their success comes from their contact with the Absolute Being. All these point to the same direction that in their management they understand the need for a proper faith and a life in accordance with it. This is the final conclusion of this research study.

This conclusion may raise certain questions in the minds of the readers. First of all there is possibility of the question why only Christian leaders were taken as examples from recent history of the world? Does it mean that only Christian faith is able to contribute for successful management? The two examples I took are from the Catholic world. This may raise a question in the minds of the non Catholic Christians namely "Do you think that Catholic faith alone brings success in management"?

These questions may be answered in the following way. Any person makes a research from his/her own stand point. One's own stand point or the area of one's personal experience is the most feasible area to start with. The first and foremost justification for my choosing these two leaders as examples is that they were the people who influenced my life as a Catholic and these were the two people about whose lives I had more information than any one else.

Secondly there is a question whether only Christian faith or Catholic faith in particular is able to bring about success in management? This is a question that lies beyond the scope of this research paper. All that I say is that Christian faith is able to bring about success in management. But whether the faith of other people is able to do the same is a question that is to be tackled by pure theology and not by the study of management. That study is beyond my scope. By selecting two Christian leaders as example I only affirm that faith is an important aspect in successful management. The faith I know is the Christian faith. I cannot either say anything negative or positive about other faiths because I am not an expert in that field and my concern is not theological but Management. There could be similar approaches and styles in other religious scriptures and that too needs to be identified and studied.

This thesis may also raise another question in the minds of the readers namely, "If faith can do such wonders what is the need for formal training"? My thesis is that faith should go along with formal training and not that faith alone is enough. As the saying goes "heaven helps those who help themselves", supernatural grace works upon natural qualities. This is the traditional conviction of the Christians. That is why side by side with training and education in spiritual matters the Church is engaged in formal education of a secular nature. Moreover, to deny the significance of formal education and training which have their origin in human efforts is to deny the value of the natural world and its resources. The world and all that is in it especially humans with the power of intellect and imagination are all the creations of God. Just because they have their source in God they are significant. To deny the significance of this natural world is to deny the significance of the act of creating. In other words if a person denies the world totally he is indirectly denying the creator. Therefore denial of the value of formal training affects faith itself. It distorts the faith. Therefore, we can conclude with confidence that faith does not make formal training irrelevant or unnecessary.

My insistence on the need of faith may prompt someone to ask, "Is it impossible for an atheist to be a successful manager"? To answer this question we have to ask a few counter questions. (1) What exactly is atheism? (2) How many are the real atheists? Let us take the second question first. The statistics of the world show that there are only very few who claim to be atheists.[1] If they are so few then they are negligible i.e. the practical influence they can have in the society, as atheists is negligible. But there is the first question namely what exactly is atheism. The dictionary meaning of atheism is "the belief that God does not exist."[2] But we have to distinguish between four types of atheism. There are the anti theists, the theoretical atheists, practical atheists, and the agnostics. All these people behave almost in the same way, namely, they don't practice any religion. But this is in the externals. But their positions are widely different. The common man is very often unable to distinguish between them. In common language all of them are called atheists. But they are not actually atheists in the same sense. Agnostics are people who doubt the existence of God. In practice they are neither theists nor atheists. This doubt about the existence of God makes them lead a life without attachment to any religion. Anti theists are not atheists i.e. they don't believe that there is no God. On the other hand they are afraid of God.

They think that belief in God will question their conscience when they lead a licentious life. So they want to avoid God or they are against God. The practical atheists are those who live as if there is no God. They also do not deny the existence of God on philosophical ground. If we exclude these three categories—the practical atheists, the anti theists and the agnostics—then the number of atheists proper becomes very negligible.

Thus we understand that atheists themselves, at least a vast majority of them, are not atheists proper. When they say there is no God what they mean is that they don't believe in the existence of the gods proposed by the religions especially the gods who behave very much like human beings, the gods who have all the weaknesses of man. Therefore, most of these atheists are not people who believe on philosophical ground that there is no God. This consideration also makes the number of atheists too little, almost nil.

Coming to this thesis we have to say the following. A research study is conducted to help the common man. In that process the negligible number of atheists if at all there are any atheists cannot deter us. In other words the existence, if at all any, of the atheists does not defeat our conclusion.

To go back to the findings of this research, the contribution of scientific management is invaluable. In this regard the contribution of the 7-S approach is specially commendable. But the 7-S approach is to be aided by what lies beyond it namely a proper faith in the Absolute Being and a life in accordance with it. This was the beauty of the life of the two characters we have taken as examples from the Bible. This is what is proved by the wonderful success of the two leaders taken from the recent world history. Seven-S approach is a valid approach, but there is need to go beyond and what lies beyond is **faith**.

Family style of leadership practised by Jesus is strongly advocated for every form of organisation be it big, or small, service or business because it has universal validity, and is a time tested and empirically justifiable one. While selecting the managers, organisations should see that the managers have also human qualities like faith in human values along with the academic fitness. Management principles based on human relations and human values have universal validity and needs greater priority than pure industry or output based principles.

REFERENCES

1. Sathyadeepam, "Technologyaeckal Kudhippu Dhaiwa Vishwasathinu", January 4, 2006, p. 7. This is written according to a survey conducted by an Agency in America called 'Haris'. The Survey Reveals that more than 82 per cent of the people have faith in God.

2. A.S. Hornby, Oxford Advanced Learner's Dictionary, (6th edn.) Great Clarendon Street, Oxford, Oxford University Press, 2000.

Bibliography

Books on Management Studies

Ackoff, R.L and E.L. Arnoff. *Introduction to Operations Research*. New York: John Wiley and Sons, 1957.

Adler, N.J. *International Dimensions of Organisational Behaviour*. Boston: PWS-Kent, 1991.

Adler, N.J and F. Ghadar. *Strategic Human Resource Management in International Comparison*. Berlin: de Gruyter, 1990.

Adorno, T. and Others. *The Authoritarian Personality*. New York: Harper and Brothers, 1950.

Aguilar, F.J. *General Managers in Action*. Oxford: Oxford University Press, 1988.

Albers, H. and H. Richard. *Cases and Incidents on the Basic Concept of Management*. New York: John Wiley and Sons, 1972.

Aldag, R. and B. Arthur. *Task Design and Employee Motivation*. Glenview, III.: Scott, F & Co., 1979.

Allison, G.T. *Essence of Decision*. Boston: Little, Brown, 1971.

Almond, G. and S. Verba. *The Civic Culture: Political Attitudes and Democracy in Five Nations*. Princeton: Princeton University Press, 1976.

Ansoff, H.I. *Implanting Strategic Management*. Englewood Cliffs, N.J.: Prentice-Hall International, 1984.

Anthony A. D'Souza, *Leaders for Today Hope for Tomorrow*, Mumbai, Pauline Publications, 2001.

Argyris, C. *Integrating the Individual and the Organisation*. New York: John Wiley, 1964.

Argyris, C. *Personality and Organisation*. New York: Harper and Row, 1957.

Athos, A. and G. John. *Interpersonal Behaviour*. Englewood Cliffs, N.J.: Prentice-Hall, 1978.

Axelrod, R. *Structure of Decision*. Princeton, N.J.: Princeton University Press, 1976.

Babbage, C. *On the Economy of Machinery and Manufacturers*, London: Charles Knight, 1832.

Balu, P.M and R.A. Schoenherr. *The Structure of Organisations*. New York: Basic Books, 1971.

Banerjee, S. *Principles and Practice of Management*. New Delhi: Oxford & IBH Publishing Co., 1994.

Bartlett, C.A. and S. Goshal. *Managing Across Borders: The Transitional Solution*. London: London Business School, 1991.

Bartlett, C.A. and S. Goshal. *Multinational Management, the Transitional Solution*. Homewood, IL: Irwin, 1992.

Beaty, J. *The World According to Drucker*. Great Britain: Orion Business Books, 1998.

Beer, S. *Decision and Control*. New York: John Wiley and Sons, 1966.

Benedict, R. *Patterns of Culture*. Boston: Houghton Mifflin, 1934.

Bernard, C.I. *The Functions of Executive*. Cambridge, Massachussetts: Harvard University Press, 1938.

Billsberry, J. *The Effective Manager*. London: Sage Publications, 1996.

Biles, G.E. and R.S. Schuler. *Audit Handbook of Human Resource Practices: Auditing the Effectiveness of the Human Resource Functions*. Alexandria, V.A: American Society for Personal Administration, 1986.

Black, J.S., H.B. Gregersen, and M. Mendenhall. *Global Assignments*. San Francisco: Jossey-Bass, 1992.

Blake, R.R. and J.S. Mouton. *The Managerial Grid*. Houston: Gulf Publishing, 1964.

Brewster, C. and A. Hegewisch, eds. *Policy and Practice in European Human Resource Management*. London: Routledge, 1994.

Brewster, C. and S. Tyson. *International Comparisons in Human Resource Management*. London: Pitman, 1991.

Buckley, P.J. and M.C. Casson. *The Future of the Multinational Enterprise*. London: Macmillan, 1976.

Burack, E.H. *Organisation Analysis: Theory and Applications*. Hinsdale, III: The Dryden Press, 1975.

Burns, T. and G.M. Stalker. *The Management of Innovation*. London: Tavistock Publications, 1961.

Burton, G. and M.Thakur. *Management Today*. New Delhi: Tata McGraw-Hill Publishing Company, 1996.

Byars, and L. Lloyd. *Strategic Management*. New York: Harper Collins Publishers, 1991.

Campbell, D.C. and R.L.Rowan. *Multinational Enterprises and the OECD Industrial Relations Guidelines*. Philadelphia: Industrial Research Unit, University of Pennsylvania, 1983.

Chakraborty, S.K. *Management by Values*. New Delhi: Oxford University Press, 1993.

Champion, J. and J. John. *Critical Incidents in Management*. Homewood, III.: Richard D. Irwin, 1975.

Chandan, J.S. *Management Concepts and Strategies*. New Delhi: Vikas Publishing House Pvt. Ltd., 1997.

Chandler, A.D. Jr. *Strategy and Structure*. Cambridge, Mass.: MIT Press, 1962.

Cole, G.A. *Management Theory and Practice*. London: DP Publications, 1996.

Cortada, J.W. *21st Century Business: Managing and Working in the New Digital Economy*. London: Prentice Hall, 2001.

Covey, S.R. *Principle Centred Leadership*. London: Pocket Books, 2002.

Culbert, S.A. and J.A. McDonough. *The Invisible War: Pursuing Self Interests at Work*. New York: John Wiley, 1980.

Daft, R.L. *Organisation Theory and Design* (7th edn.). U.S.A.: South-Western Thomson Learning, 2001.

Dale, M. *Developing Management Skills, Techniques for Improving Learning and Performance*. London: Kogan Page, 2003.

Davidson, M. *The Transformation of Management*. London: Macmillan Press Ltd., 1995.

Davis, K. *Human Behaviour at Work*: *Organisational Behaviour* (6th edn.). New York: McGraw-Hill, 1981.

Davis, R.C. *The Fundamentals of Top Management*. New York: Harper & Row, Pub., 1957.

Dessler, G. *Organization and Management*. Reston, Va. :Reston, 1982.

Dessler, G. *Management Fundamentals; Modern Principles and Practices* (4th edn.). Reston, Virginia: Prentice-Hall Co., 1985.

Donnelly, J.H., J.L. Gibson and J.M. Ivancevich. *Fundamentals of Management*. Massachussetts.: Irwin McGraw-Hill, 1998.

Drucker, P.F. *The Practice of Managemnt*. London: William Heinemann Ltd., 1969.

Drucker, P.F. *Management: Task, Responsibilities, Practices.* New York: Harper & Row, Pub., 1973.

Drucker, P.F. *Management Challenges for the 21st Century.* Oxford: Butterworth Heinemann, 1999.

England, G.W. *The Manager and the Man.* Kent, OH: Kent State University Press, 1974.

England, G.W. *The Manager and His Values.* Cambridge, MA: Ballinger, 1975.

Erez, M. and P.C. Earley. *Culture, Self-identity, and Work.* New York: Oxford University Press, 1993.

Farmer, R. and Others. *Incidents in Applying Management Theory.* Belmon.: Calif. Wadswort, 1966.

Fayol, H. *General and Industrial Administration.* New York: Pitman Publishing Corporation, 1949.

Fiedler, F.E. *A Theory of Leadership Effectiveness.* New York: McGraw-Hill, 1967.

Follett, M.P. *The Speaker of the Use of Representative,* New York: Longman, 1909.

Follett, M.P. *The New State,* New York: Longman, 1920.

Follett, M.P. *Creative Experience,* New York: Longman, 1924.

Follett, M.P. *Business Management As a Profession,* (ed) H.C. Metcalf, Chicago: A. W. Shaw and Company, 1927.

Follett, M.P. *Dynamic Administration: The Collected Papers of Mary Parker Follett, (ed)* M. Metcalf and L. Urwick, London: Pitman, 1941.

Follett, M.P. *Freedom and Coordination: Lectures in Business Organisation* by Mary Parker Follett, (ed) L. Urwick, London: Pitman, 1949.

Forrester, J.W. *Industrial Dynamics.* New York: The MIT Press & John Wiley and Sons, 1961.

Gantt, H.L. *Works, Wages and Profits.* New York: Engineering Magazine Col., 1910.

Gantt, H.L. *Industrial Leadership*. New Haven: Yale University Press, 1916.

Gantt, H.L. *Organising for Work*. New York: Har Court Brace and Howe, 1919.

George, C.H. *The Human Group*. New York: Har Court Brace and Company, 1950.

George, C.S. Jr. *The History of Management Thought* (2nd edn.). Englewood Cliffs, N.J.: Prentice-Hall, 1972.

Ghiselli, E.E. *Exploration In Managerial Talent*. Pacific Press, Calif.: Goodyear, 1971.

Gilbreth, F.B. (Jr.) and E.G.Carey. *Cheaper by the Dozen*. New York: Thomas Y. Crowell, 1971.

Gilbreth, F.B. (Jr.) *Time Out for Happiness*. New York: Thomas Y. Crowell, 1971.

Glueck, W.F. *Business Policy: Strategy Formation and Executive Action*. New York: McGraw-Hill, 1972.

Gupta, N.K. and A. Ahamad. *Managing Transition*. New Delhi: Wiley Eastern Limited, 1994.

Haire, M. E.E. Ghiselli, and L.W. Porter. *Managerial Thinking: An International Study*. New York: Wiley, 1966.

Hampton, D.R. *Management* (3rd ed.).New York: McGraw-Hill Book Company, 1987.

Hannagan, T. *Management Concepts and Practices*. Delhi: Macmillan India Ltd, 1997.

Harrison, E.F. *The Managerial Decision-Making Process* (2nd ed.). Boston: Houghton Miflin Co., 1981.

Harris P. and R. Moran. *Managing Cultural Differences*. Houston, Texas: Gulf Publishing Co., 1979.

Heenan, D.A and H.V. Perlmutter. *Multinational Organisation Development*. Reading, M.A: Addison-Wesley, 1979.

Hennart, J.F. *A Theory of the Multinational Enterprise*. Ann Arbor: University of Michigan Press, 1982.

Heller, R. & T. Hindle. *Essential Manager's Manual*. London: Dorling Kindersley, 1998.

Hofstede, G. *Culture's Consequences: International Differences in Work-Related Values*. Beverly Hills, CA: Sage Publications, 1980.

Homans, G.C. *The Human Group*. New York: Harcourt Brace and Company, 1950.

Humble, J.W. *Improving Business Results*. Maidenhead, England: McGraw-Hill Book Company, 1968.

Jackson, T. *Organisational Behaviour in International Management*. Oxford: Butterworth-Heinemann Ltd, 1993.

Jevons, W.S. *The Theory of Political Economy*. New York: The McMillan Company. 1888.

Jorgensen, D.L. *Participant Observation: A Methodology for Human Studies*. Newbury Park, C.A.: Sage Publications, 1989.

Justis, R. *Dynamics of American Business*. Englewood Cliffs, N.J.: Prentice-Hall, 1982.

Katz, K.and R.L.Kahn. *The Social Psychology of Organisations* (2nd ed.). New York: John Wiley, 1978.

Khandelwal, N.M. *Management Concepts From the Mahabharatha*, Delhi: New Century Publications, 2001.

Knapper, A. *Cases in Personal Management*. Columbus: Grid, 1977.

Koch, R. *The Financial Times Guide to Strategy: How to Create and Deliver a Useful Strategy*. London: Pearson Education Ltd, 1995.

Koontz, H. and H. Weihrich. *Management*. New York: McGraw-Hill Publishing Co., 1988.

Koontz, H. *Appraising Managers as Managers*. New York: McGraw-Hill Book Company, 1971.

Kuhn, T. *The Structure of Scientific Revolutions* (2nd ed.). Chicago, IL: University of Chicago Press, 1970.

Lawrence, P. and J.W. Lorsch. *Organisation and Environment: Managing Differentiation and Integration*. Boston: Harvard Business School, Division of Research, 1967.

Leontiades, M. *Management Policy, Strategy and Plans*. Boston: Little Brown, 1982.

Likert, R. *New Patterns of Management*. New York: McGraw-Hill Book Company, 1961.

Locke, E.A. and G.P. Latham. *A Theory of Goal Setting and Task Performance*. Englewood Cliffs, N.J.: Prentice-Hall, 1990.

Lorange, P. *Corporate Planning*. Englewood Cliffs, N.J.: Prentice-Hall, 1980.

McKenzie, K. *Organisational Structure*. Arlington Heights, III.: AHM, 1978.

Martin, J. *Cultures in Organisations: Three Perspectives*. New York: Oxford University Press, 1993.

Maslow, A. *Motivation and Personality*. New York: Harper & Row, Pub., 1954.

Massie, L.J. *Essentials of Management*, New Delhi: Prentice Hall of India Pvt. Ltd., 1976.

Massie, J.L. and Douglas, J. *Managing: A Contemporary Introduction*. Englewood Cliffs, N.J.: Prentice-Hall, 1983.

Mayo, E. *The Political Problem of an Industrial Society*. Cambridge: Harvard University, 1947.

McCelland, D.C. *The Achieving Society*. Princeton, N.J.: Van Nostrand, 1961.

McGregor, D. *The Human Side of Enterprise*. New York: McGraw-Hill, 1960.

Melcher, A. *Structure and Process of Organisation*. Englewood Cliffs, N.J.: Prentice-Hall, 1976.

Michael, V.P. Management for Managers, Bombay: Himalaya Publishing House, 1992.

Michael, V.P. *Perspective Management*. Bombay: Himalaya Publishing House, 1994.

Mill, J. *Elements of Political Economy*. London: Baldwin Cradock and Joy. 1826.

Mill, J.S. *Principles of Political Economy*, (ed) Sir W.J. Ashley. London: Longmans, 1826.

Miner, J.B. *Theories of Organisational Behaviour*. Hinsdale, III.: Dryden Press, 1980.

Mintzberg, H. *The Nature of Managerial Work*. New York: Harper & Row, Pub., 1973.

Mintzberg, H. *Structuring of Organisations*. Englewood Cliffs, N.J.: Prentice-Hall, 1979.

Mintzberg, H. *Structure in Fives: Designing Effective Organisations*. Englewood Cliffs, N.J.: Prentice-Hall, 1983.

Moorhead, G. and R.Griffin. *Organisational Behaviour*. Boston: Houton, 1969.

Moorthy, K.K. *Management Philosophy for the New Millennium*. New Delhi: Allied Publishers Ltd, 2001.

Ouchi, W.G. *Theory Z: How American Business Can Meet the Japanese Challenge*. Reading, Mass.: Addison-Wesley, 1981.

Owen, R. *Socialism: A Primary Source Analysis*. Amazon: The Rosen Publishing Group, 1858.

Pascale, R.T. and A.G.Athos. *The Art of Japanese Management*. New York: Penguin Books. 1981.

Perrow, C. *Organisational Analysis: A Sociological Perspective*. Belmont, Calif.: Wadsworth, 1970.

Peter, L.J. *The Peter Principle*. London: Penguin. 1970.

Peters, T.J. and R.H. Waterman (Jr.). *In Search of Excellence*. New York: Harper & Row, 1982.

Petrick, J.A. and Quinn, J.F. *Management Ethics*. New Delhi: Response Books, 1997.

Pettinger, R. *Introduction to Management*. New York, Palgrave, 2002.

Pfeffer, Jeffrey. *Organisational Design*. Arlington Heights, III.: AHM Publishing Corp., 1978.

Phatak, A.V. *International Dimensions of Management* (3rd ed.). Boston: PWS-Kent. 1992.

Pike, R. *Language in Relation to a United Theory of the Structure of Human Behaviour*. Glendale, AZ: Summer Institute of Linguistics. 1954.

Poole, M. *Industrial Relations: Origins and Patterns of National Diversity*. London: Routledge & Kegan Paul. 1986.

Porter, M. *Competitive Strategy: Techniques for Analysing Industries and Competitors*. New York: Free Press, 1980.

Porter, M.E. *Competition in Global Industries*. Boston: Harvard Business School Press. 1986.

Porter, M.E. *Competitive Advantage of Nations*. New York: Free Press. 1990.

Prasad, L. and S.S. Gulshan. *Management Principles and Practices*. New Delhi: S. Chand & Company Ltd. 1982.

Prasad, L.M. *Principles and Practice of Management*. New Delhi: Sultan Chand & Sons. 1979.

Punnett, B.J. & O. Shenkar. *Handbook for International Management Research*. New Delhi: Beacon Books. 1998.

Punnett, B.J. and D.A. Ricks. *International Business*. Boston: PWS-Kent. 1992.

Rachman, D. and M. Mescon. *Business Today*. New York: Random House. 1979.

Ramasamy, T. *Principles of Management*. New Delhi. Himalaya Publishing House, 2003.

Rasiel, E.M. *The McKenzie Way* (3rd ed.). New Delhi: Tata McGraw—Hill Publishing Company Limited 2003.

Rasiel E.M. and P.N. Friga. The McKenzie Mind. New Delhi: Tata McGraw – Hill Publishing Company Limited. 2003.

Reddin, W.J. *Managerial Effectiveness*. New York: McGraw Hill, Inc. 1970.

Richard, N. *Service Management* (3rd ed.). New York: John Wiley & Sons, Ltd. 2000.

Richman, B.M. and R.N. Farmer. *Leadership, Goals and Power in Higher Education.* San Francisco: Jossey-Bass. 1974.

Robbins, S.P. Personnel: *The Management of Human Resources* (2nd ed.). Englewood Cliffs, NJ.: Prentice-Hall. 1982.

Robbins, S.P. *Management: Concepts and Practices.* Englewood Cliffs, NJ.: Prentice-Hall, Inc. 1984.

Robbins, S.P. *Organisational Behaviour.* New Delhi: Prentice Hall of India. 1993.

Rohner, R. *They Love, They Move Me Not.* New Haven, CT: HRAF Press. 1975.

Ronen, S. *Comparative and Multinational Management.* New York: Wiley & Sons. 1986.

Runkel, P.J. and J.E. McGrath. *Research on Human Behaviour: A Systematic Guide to Method.* New York: Holt: Rinehart and Winston. 1972.

Sadri, S. and Others. *The Theory and Practice of Managerial Ethics*, Mumbai: Jaico Publishing House, 1999.

Samuel, P.N. *Elements of Political Economy.* Andover: Gould and Newman. 1835.

Say, J.B. *Catechism of Political Economy.* London: Sherwood, 1816.

Schein, E.H. *Organisational Culture and Leadership: A Dynamic View.* San Francisco: Jossey-Bass. 1985.

Sethi, S.P. and R. Hilton. *The Management of Multinationals.* New York: The Free Press, 1974.

Sharma, A.K. *Motivational Dynamics.* Jaipur: Rawat Publications. 1990.

Sheldon, O. *The Philosophy of Management.* New York: Pitman. 1966.

Simon, H.A. *Models of Man*. New York: John Wiley. 1957.

Simon, H.A. *The New Science of Management Decision*. New York: Harper & Row, Pub. 1960.

Simon, H.A . *Administrative Behavior* (3rd ed.). New York: Free Press. 1976.

Singh, N.K and O. Paul. *The Corporate Soul*. New Delhi: Vision. 1985.

Singh, R.N. *Management Thought and Thinkers*. New Delhi: Sultan Chand & Sons, 1977.

Sinha, J.C and V.N. Mugali. *Business Management*. New Delhi: R.C. Chand & Co. 1977.

Smith, A. *An Enquiry into the Nature and Causes of Wealth of the Nations*. London: A Straham and T. Cadell, 1793.

Steiner, G.A. *Strategic Planning: What Every Manager Must Know*. New York: Free Press. 1981.

Steiner, G.A., J.B. Miner, and E.R. Gray. *Management Policy and Strategy* (3rd ed.). New York: The Macmillan Publishing Company. 1986.

Stogdill, R.M. *Handbook of Leadership: A Survey of Theory and Research*. New York: Free Press. 1974.

Tannenbaum, A.S. *Control in Organisations*. New York: McGraw-Hill. 1968.

Taylor, F.W. *Scientific Management*. New York: Harper & Row, 1947.

Terry, G.R. and S.G. Franklin. *Principles of Management*. New Delhi: All India Traveller Book Seller. 1991.

Thompson, J.D. *Organisations in Action*. New York: McGraw-Hill. 1967.

Tripathy, P.C. and P.N. Reddy. *Principles of Management*. New Delhi: Tata McGraw-Hill Publishing Co. 1993.

Tuggle, F.D. *Organisational Processes*. Arlington Heights, III.: AHM Publishing Corp. 1978.

Tuteja, S.K. (Editor). *Management Mosaic*. New Delhi: Excel Books, 2005.

Urwick, L.F. *The Elements of Administration*. London:Pitman, 1947.

Vroom, V.H. *Work and Motivation*. New York: John Wiley. 1964.

Walter, C.P. and B. Sparkes. *Life of an American Workman*. New York: Dodd, Mead & Co. 1950.

Weihrich, H. *Management Excellence—Productivity Through MBO*. New York: McGraw-Hill Book Company. 1985.

Wexley, K. and G. Yukl. *Organisational Behaviour and Personal Psychology*. Homewood, III.: Richard D. Irwin. 1977.

Wexley, K. and G. Latham. *Developing and Training Human Resources in Organisations*. Glenview: Scott, Forseman. 1981.

Womack, S., P. Jones and J. Roos. *The Machine That Changed the World*. New York: Society of Mechanical Engineers. 1990.

Woodward, Joan. *Industrial Organisation: Theory and Practice*. London: Oxford University Press. 1965.

Wren, D. *The Evaluation of Management Thought*. New York: The Ronald Press Co. 1972.

Yoder, D. *Personnel Management and Industrial Relations*. Englewood Cliffs, N.J.: Prentice-Hall. 1970.

Periodicals on Management Studies

British Journal of Management, Blackwell Publishing, U.K.

Business Week, The McGraw Hill Companies, New York

Business World, Express Building, Bahadur Shah Zafar Marg, New Delhi.

Business Today, Pavan Varshnei, Delhi.

California Management, University of California, Berkeley.

Fortune, Rockefeller Center, New York.

Harvard Business Review, Harvard Business School Publishing Corporation, Boston, Canada.

Human Resource Management, John Wiley & Sons, III River Street, England.

Human Relations, Sage Publications Limited, London.

HRM Review, ICFAI University Press, Hyderabad.

Indian Management, Nehru House, 4 Bahadur Shah Zafar Marg, New Delhi.

Indian Management Studies, Punjab School of Management Studies, Punjab University, Patiala.

India Today, Harper Collins, New Delhi.

International Journal of Management Literature, Spellbound Publications Pvt. Ltd., Delhi.

Journal of Applied Management Studies, Carfax Publishing, U.K.

Journal of General Management, The Braybrooke Press Ltd, U.K.

Journal of Management History, Nova Southern University, Fort Lauderdale, Florida, USA.

Journal of Management Research, PSG Institute of Management, Coimbatore.

Journal of Management Studies, Blackwell Publishing Company, U.K.

Management Today, Australia Institute of Management, Australia.

People Management, Chartered Institute Personnel and Development (CIPD), U.K.

Rajagiri Management Journal, Rajagiri School of Management, Kochi.

Sales and Marketing Management, Bill Communications, New York.

Strategic Management Journal, John Wiley & Sons, England.

25. *The TQM Magazine*, MCB University Press, ISSN.

Books on Biblical Studies

Albright, W.F. and C.S Mann. *Mathew, A New Translation with Introduction and Commentary. The Anchor Bible.* New York: Doubleday, 1971.

Boff, C. and G.V. Pixley. *The Bible, the Church and the Poor.* Maryknoll, New York: Orbis Books, 1993.

Boff, L. *Jesus Christ Liberator: A Critical Christology for our Time.* New York: Orbis Books, 1997.

Briner, B. and R. Pritchard. *The Leadership Lessons of Jesus: A Timeless Model for Today's Leaders.* Nashville, Tennessee: Broadman & Holman Publishers, 1997.

Brown, R.E. *The Gospel According to John 1-XII, A New Translation with Introduction. The Anchor Bible.* New York: Doubleday, 1966.

Brown, R.E. *The Gospel According to John XIII-XXI, A New Translation with Introduction. The Anchor Bible.* New York: Doubleday, 1970.

Clements, R.E. *A Century of Old Testament Study.* London: Lutterworth Press, 1992.

Coats, G.W. *The Moses Tradition.* Sheffield, JSOT Press, 1993.

Collins, J.J. "The Exodus and Biblical Theology", *Biblical Theological Bulletin.* Vol. 25, 1995.

Desrochers, J. *Christ The Liberator.* Bangalore: The Centre for Social Action, 1997.

Ellis, P.F. *The Men and Message of the Old Testament.* Collegeville: Liturgical Press, 1962.

Geldenhuys, N. *The Gospel of Luke: The New International Commentary on the New Testament, Michigan*: M.M.B. Eerdmans, 1988.

Gnilka, J. *Jesus of Nazareth: Message and History.* USA: Hendrickson, 1997.

Gottwald, N.K. and R.A. Horsely (Editors). *The Bible and Liberation: Political and Social Hermeneutics*, Maryknoll, New York: Orbis Books, 1993.

Gula, R.M. *What are They Saying About Moral Norms?* New York: Paulist Press, 1981.

Gustafson, J.M. *Christ and the Moral Life*. New York: Harper and Row, 1968.

Heney, D. *Concrete Leadership Strategies for Pastors, Administrators and Lay Leaders*. Mumbai: Pauline Publications, 2000.

Jacobs-Malina, D. *"Gender, Power, and Jesus' Identity in the Gospels"*, Biblical Theology Bulletin. Vol. 24 (1994). No. 4.

Jegen, C.F. *Restoring Our Friendship With God: The Mystery of Redemption From Suffering and Sin*. Wilmington: Michael Glazier (Publisher), 1989.

Johnson, S.E. *Jesus and His Town*. Wilmington: Michael Glazier, 1989.

John, E. *A Christian Perspective of Management*. Chennai, Dr. Easo John Associates, 2003.

Jones, L.B. *JESUS CEO: Using Ancient Wisdom for Visionary Leadership*. New York, Hyperion, 1994.

Jones, L.B. *Jesus Entrepreneur*, New York, Three Rivers Press, 2001.

Kealy, S.P. *Jesus and Politics*. Collegeville, Minnesota: The Liturgical Press, 1990.

Klagsbrun, F. *The Story of Moses*. London: Flanklin Watts, 1968.

Koester, H. *Ancient Christian Gospels*. Cambridge, Massachussetts: Trinity Press International, 1990.

Mann, C.S. *Mark. New Translation with Introduction and Commentary*—The Anchor Bible Series. New York: Doubleday, 1986.

McKenzie, J.L. *Dictionary of the Bible*. London: Geoffrey Chapman, 1975.

Nogar, R.J. *Evolution Organic, New Catholic Encyclopaedia*, Vol. 5.

Olson, H.A. *Power Strategies of Jesus Christ*, New York, Triumph Books, 1991.

Pawlikowski, J. *Jesus and the Theology of Israel*. Wilmington, Delaware: Michael Glazier, Inc. 1989.

Pfeiffer, C.F. *Old Testament History*. Grand Rapids: Baker Book House, 1973.

Pixley, G.V. *On Exodus: A Liberation Perspective*. Maryknoll, New York: Orbis Books, 1993.

Rowley, H.H. (ed). *Old Testament and Modern Study*. Oxford: Oxford University Press, 1951.

Schultz, S.J. *The Gospel of Moses*: Moody Press, Chicago, 1979 p. 68.

Index

A

Abraham offspring, 114
Akande, Adebowale, 5
American enterprises, 75
Approaches to management, 53-75
    case approach, 54
    composite Longwall method approach, 59-60
    contingency approach, 65-66
    co-operative social systems approach, 58-59
    decision making role, 68
    – theory approach, 61
    disseminator role, 67-68
    disturbance handler role, 68
    entrepreneurial role, 68
    figurehead role, 67
    group behaviour approach, 56-58
informational roles, 67
    inter-personal behaviour approach, 55-56
    interpersonal roles, 67
    leader role, 67
    liaison role, 67
    management process approach, 70-71
    managerial roles approach, 66
    negotiator role, 69-70
    quantitative or mathematical approach to management, 64
    recipient role, 67
    resource allocator role, 68
    spokesperson role, 68
    systems approach, 61-64
Attributes, 77
Authority and responsibility, 22
Autonomy and entrepreneurship, 78
Awareness, 63

B

Babbagge, Charles, 16
Baron, Rabbi, 8
Beyond seven-S, 158-172
    beyond in the Biblical management, 167
    limitations, 159
    recognition of the divine in the human, 164-165
Bias for action, 78
Bible, 3

C

Carnegie, Dale, 29
Centralisation and decentralisation, 23
Christian movement, 1
Close to the customer, 78
Corporate strategies, 81-82
Cotton, Charles, 83

D

D'Souza, Anthony A., 9
Discipline, 23
Division of work, 22

E

Edgeman, Rick L., 7
Egyptian rules, 121
Emphasis on human relationship in management, 26
Entrepreneur, 7
Equity, 24
Esprit de corps, 24
Exodus movement, 103

F

Follett, Mary Parker, 28
Franklin, S.G., 55

G

God of Abraham, 106
God of Isaac, 106
God of Jacob, 106
Gospel of Mark, 129, 131

H

Hands-on, value driven, 78
Harappa, 14
Herzberg, Frederick, 39

I

Initiative, 24
Integrated management thought, 45
Interpersonal skill, 96

J

Jerusalem, 139
Jesus, 3, 7, 127-157
Jewish people, 2
Jones, Laurie Beth, 6

K

Katz, Daniel, 40
Kennedy, Michael Henry, 8
Khan, Robert, 40
Khandelwal, N.M., 8
Kingdom of God, 128, 129, 133
Koontz, H., 56

L

Leadership styles in the Jesus movement, 141
Lewin, Kurt, 41, 42
Likert, Rensis, 38

M

Management as a science by itself, 43
Management Process School, 25
Manager functions, 66
Market Expansion Corporate Strategy, 82
Mayo, Elton, 27
McCormick, Donald W., 6
Metanoeo, 131
Michael, V.P., 12
Mintzberg, Henry, 66
Mohanjadhara, 14
Mosaic authority, 111
Moses, 2, 3, 103-110, 117, 121

N

New Testament, 2, 1, 101, 126, 131, 151

O

Obserholster, Braam, 5
Ohmae, Kenichi, 84
Old Testament, 2, 1, 101, 151
Order, 24

P

Paternalism, 111
Perspective systems, 87
Peter, Lawrence J., 29
Peters, Tom, 77
Pettinger, Richard, 76
Pharaoh, 104
Pheng, Low Sui, 8
Plympian corporate strategy, 81
Praising employees, 96
Productivity through people, 78

R

Remuneration, 23
Roethlisberger, 27

S

Sabbath observance, 108
Scalar chain, 24
Scaperlanda, Anthony, 7
Schools of management thought, 10
  beginnings, 14-16
  Fayol, Henri, 22
  first stage, 16-18
  five stages of development, 14
  Gantt, Henry Laurence, 21
  Gilbreth, Frank Bunker, 21
  Gilbreth, Lillian Moller, 21
  management and administration, 11-14
  some important contributors in the first stage, 18
  Taylor, Frederic Winslow, 19-21
Seven -S approach, 3, 4, 74-100
  concept of excellence, 76-78
  different items in the 7-S approach, 79
  in the Bible, 101-126
    Aaron, 115-116
getting the people out of Egypt, 104-106
god, 114-115
in the liberation movement of moses, 102-103
mediating a covenant between god and the people, 107
Moses, 115
preservation of the status, 107-108
seventy elders, 116-121
shared value, 121-122
skills, 122-124
staff, 113-114
strategy, 103-104
structure, 104
style, 109-113
system, 108-109
Jesus movement, 153
life of Jesus, 127-157
approach to the staff, 148-150
god, 142
Jesus, 142-143
seventy disciples, 145
shared values, 150-152
skills, 152-154
staff, 142
strategy of Jesus, 127-131
structure, 131-133
style, 138-141
system, 133-138
to be sent out, 144-145
to be with him, 143-144
to have authority to cast out demons, 145
twelve apostles, 143
women, 146-148

researches leading to 7-S approach. 75-76
shared values. 93-94
skills. 95-97
staff, 91
confrontational approach, 92-93
cooperative approach, 92
mutual approach, 92
plural approach. 91
radical approach. 91-92
unitary approach. 91
structure, 84-86
style. 88
autocratic or authoritarian style. 88
consultative or participative style. 88
democratic style. 88-89
expert style. 89-91
manipulative style. 89
nureaucratic style. 89
paternalistic style. 89
system, 86-87
what business are you in, 82
what criteria can you use to measure your performance, 83-84
Short history of management thought, 1-52
literature relating management with religion and spirituality. 5-10
methodology, 4-5
objectives of the study, 3-4
Simple from, lean staff, 79
Simultaneous loose-tight properties, 79
Situational approach, 85
Social sciences and management, 30
Argyris, Chris, 34
authority, 36-37
Bernard, Chester I., 35
classification of organisation, 36
concept of organisation, 36
contingency theory, 46
elements of organisation, 36
executive leadership, 37
functions of executive, 37
Herzberg. Frederick. 39
Maslow. Abraham, 33
McGregor. Douglas, 31
motivation. 37
organisational equilibrium, 37
systems theory. 46-47
Spiritreneurism. 7
Stability of job tenure. 24
Staff in the Jesus movement. 147
Staff of Jesus movement. 149
Stick to the knitting, 78
Stone, Gregory, 9
Subordination of individual interest to group interest or organisational interest. 23
System approach, 62, 63

T

Taylor, F.W., 19
Terry, G.R., 55
The Art of Japanese Management. 76
Theory Z of William Ouchi. 33
Training programme, 96

U

Unity of command, 23
Unity of direction, 23

W

Weihrich, H., 56

❑❑❑